Wetland Planting Guide for the Northeastern United States

Plants for Wetland
Creation, Restoration, and Enhancement

by
Gwendolyn A. Thunhorst

Illustrated by
Dawn R. Biggs
and
Britt Eckhardt Slattery

P.O. Box P
210 West Chew Avenue
St. Michaels, Maryland 21663
(410) 745-9620

D1260049

Published by Environmental Concern Inc.
P.O. Box P
210 West Chew Ave.
St. Michaels, Maryland 21663

Environmental Concern Inc. is a non-profit corporation devoted to the research, development, and application of technology in the restoration and construction of wetlands.

Although the author and publisher have conducted exhaustive research to ensure the accuracy and completeness of the information contained in this book, we assume no responsibility for errors, inaccuracies, omissions or any inconsistency herein.

Printed in the United States of America

CONTENTS

ACKNOWLEDGEMENTS

I am extremely indebted to Dr. Edgar Garbisch for his contribution to this guide as well as for his guidance during my time at Environmental Concern. Thanks to Britt Slattery who provided technical review and invaluable assistance in editing this document. I would also like to thank the staff at E.C. including Donald MacLean, Suzanne McIninch, Dr. Candy Bartoldus, Joanna Garbisch, Robbin Bergfors, Dr. Mark Kraus, and Mark Schilling for all of their technical and editorial support.

The information provided by other professionals working on a day to day basis with the plants in this guide was invaluable. I would especially like to thank Dr. Gary Pierce at Southern Tier Consulting, Inc. and JoAnn Gillespie at Country Wetlands Nursery, Ltd. Information provided by Dr. Aimlee Laderman at the School of Forestry at Yale University; David Donnelly at Molzon Landscape Nursery; Mike Hollins at Envirens, Inc. and many nursery owners and managers was also extremely helpful.

HOW TO USE THIS GUIDE

Introduction

As activities within wetlands have become more regulated, compensation of wetland loss has become increasingly necessary. While the science is expanding rapidly, much remains to be learned about most aspects of wetland creation, restoration, and enhancement. Vegetative characteristics are no exception. With each project, information about plant tolerances is obtained. Surprisingly little of this new knowledge is published and that which is remains difficult for wetland designers to access.

This guide is an effort to consolidate the information available from many different sources on wetland species from the northeastern United States. The U.S. Fish and Wildlife Service defines the Northeast Region (Region 1) to include: Maine, New Hampshire, Vermont, Massachusetts, Connecticut, Rhode Island, New York, New Jersey, Pennsylvania, Delaware, Maryland, District of Columbia, Virginia, Ohio, West Virginia, and Kentucky (Reed 1988). Plants which are common in wetlands in these areas are described.

It is hoped that the guide will prevent the placement of species in areas where they cannot compete or survive. It is also hoped that wetland designers will be able to use the selection of plants in this guide in order to vary the species they use, not only from project to project, but within projects, therefore duplicating natural systems more closely.

Plant Selection

Trees, shrubs, herbaceous emergent plants, and submerged or floating aquatic vegetation were chosen on the basis of their potential for successful establishment in wetland creation, restoration, and enhancement projects. Plants were identified which have been used successfully in previous projects, are recommended in other planting guides, or were carried by nurseries which deal in wetland plant materials. Species were not included if not enough information could be found to enable designers to accurately specify the plant in a wetland project. However, some species were included even if all of the information required in an information sheet was not available. For this reason, **if a piece of information appears to be left blank it should not necessarily be assumed that the section is not applicable but rather that this information was not available at the time of publication.**

An effort was made to identify species which are most commonly found in northeastern wetlands. Many of the most dominant species have been included. In the herbaceous emergent plant section, some species are included which are found in small clusters or individually throughout wetlands (i.e., they rarely dominate) with the intent that these species may add the natural diversity that many projects lack.

Plant Sheets

Four categories of vegetation are included in this guide (adapted from Tiner 1988):

- **Trees:** woody vegetation, generally over 20 feet in height

- **Shrubs:** woody vegetation, generally less than 20 feet in height

- **Herbaceous Emergent Vegetation:** non-woody vegetation, including forbs, grasses, rushes, and sedges

- **Submerged or Floating Aquatic Vegetation (SAV or FAV):** aquatic vegetation, usually submerged or floating in standing water; not standing erect out of the water

There is a Plant Sheet for each species in the guide. For the most part the sheets are set up the same way for all four types of vegetation, although small differences exist. Each sheet contains information about the species' general characteristics, its appearance, its value to wildlife, and its hydrologic tolerances. These are the traits that have been identified as useful for wetland landscape architects, designers, and planners.

Plant Names

Plants are in alphabetical order by scientific name within each category. Scientific names are verified by *A Synonymized Checklist of the Vascular Flora of the United States, Canada, and Greenland Volume II: The Biota of North America* (Kartesz and Kartesz 1980). Commonly used synonyms are provided in parentheses. Common names are given below the scientific name. Although synonyms occur for some species, scientific names are universal throughout the world, while the same species may be called by several different common names depending on region or even within a region. In addition, more than one species may be identified by the same common name. It is best to identify plants by their scientific names so that there is no confusion.

Invasive Species

Some species are known to be invasive or aggressive. Because of their rapid growth, the lack of natural competitors, and/or their allelopathic nature (**allelopathy:** the harmful effect on a plant by another plant that secretes a toxic chemical (Barnhart 1986)), invasive species may become established and take over areas beyond those for which they were intended. Invasive species can out-compete native vegetation and destroy the natural diversity of a community. For these reasons some species are prohibited from use in many areas. Species that may exhibit these characteristics are identified by a statement of caution in the upper right-hand corner of their information sheets.

Some invasive species have been included because their use has been accepted for specific purposes where other types of vegetation are not suitable. For example, some species may provide shore erosion control in high energy areas and/or water quality improvement in polluted areas. They have also been included so that designers will be aware of their invasive nature. These plants should be used only with extreme caution.

Characteristics

The **Characteristics** section of the Plant Sheet describes the general traits of a species which are important for practical design purposes. For herbaceous emergent and aquatic vegetation general characteristics are given such as whether the plant is an annual or a perennial. **Annual** plants germinate, flower, produce seed, and die within one growing season (Barnhart 1986) and reproduce only by seed. In **perennial** species, after the aboveground portions die, dormant, vegetative, belowground portions remain and sprout in the same area as last year's plants at the beginning of the new growing season. For wetland design the use of perennial plants is preferred because conditions in a wetland (e.g., water movement) tend to move seed away from the original planting area. This makes it difficult to guarantee that an annual will remain on site from year to year; however, a few annuals are included in the guide because of their other beneficial traits (e.g., wildlife value).

The persistence of the aboveground portion of herbaceous plants is also identified. At the end of the growing season **persistent** plants remain standing after dying as dry, upright stalks (e.g., *Typha spp.*, *Hibiscus moscheutos*). This quality may be beneficial by providing winter habitat or by continuing to protect a shoreline throughout the dormant season. **Semi-persistent** species may remain standing for a portion of the dormant season or do fall over but remain for part of the dormant season as dry clumps. The aboveground portion of **nonpersistent** species break down or wash away at the end of each growing season.

Trees and shrubs are identified as **broad-** or **needle-leaved** and as **deciduous** or **evergreen**. These factors can be important when considering wildlife habitat.

Growth and **Planting** information is given so that plant spacing and material can be specified. Herbaceous emergent or aquatic plants which spread rapidly by rhizomes may be expected to dominate an area in which they are planted (and sometimes beyond). Recommended on-center (OC) spacing in order to achieve ground cover appears in the suggested spacing category under planting. Species designated as having a slow rate of spread may form clumps or tussocks. If this is the case, this kind of description appears in the **Notes** section and recommended on-center spacing to achieve aerial cover appears in the suggested spacing category. Other slow spreaders do not cover large areas and are found individually or in clusters throughout wetlands and should be planted in a similar fashion, as is recommended in the suggested spacing category. These species add diversity to the wetland. Spreading rates provided are approximations and are applicable only when species are planted in deconsolidated soil.

The growth rate for woody species is given in terms of leader growth or increase in height. This can be useful if it is necessary to have a mature stand of trees within a certain period. Shrubs which are described as spreading by **stolons** send out slender stems along or beneath the surface of the ground, taking root at the tip and growing into new plants (Barnhart 1986). **Suckers** or adventitious shoots form on the trunk or branches of a tree and a new plant results (Barnhart 1986). Thickets which are valuable cover for wildlife may develop and some soil stabilization may be provided by species which spread by stolons or suckers.

Information on which **forms** of plant material are currently carried by nurseries is provided so that the designer may determine what type of material can be obtained. It is important that the designer only specify types of plant material which are available so that time and resources are not wasted trying to locate plant material that no one carries. Examples of forms or types of vegetation carried by nurseries are:

- **seed**
- **rhizome or rootstock:** rootlike, creeping, underground stem; sends out roots below and shoots above; stores food to be used by the new plant (Barnhart 1986)
- **tuber:** a solid, thickened portion or outgrowth of an underground stem, of a more or less rounded form, bearing modified axillary buds from which new plants may arise (Barnhart 1986)
- **bulb:** a round underground bud (Barnhart 1986)
- **bare root plant (growing or dormant):** an entire, usually young, plant with sediment removed/washed from roots
- **plug:** entire, usually young, plant with sediment still on roots (container or collected from the wild)
- **peat or fiber pot:** young plant in organic pot which can be placed directly into planting holes
- **container:** plants of various ages in plastic pots
- **balled and burlapped:** tree or shrub where root ball has been removed from ground and wrapped in burlap for delivery

Wetland design sometimes requires the use of specific types of material. For example, the planting of bare root woody material has not been very successful in wetland planting projects (Garbisch personal communication). Although this option is often less expensive, containerized plants are more appropriate for planting woody species in wet areas.

It is the purpose of the guide to include plants which are provided by nurseries; however, because of the important qualities of some species, others are included despite the fact that they may not be carried by nurseries. It is hoped that these plants will become available through nurseries as the demand for them increases but until then, other methods may be necessary in order to obtain these species.

In some cases it may be possible to contract a nursery to grow the required species. Proper lead time must be given if this is necessary. In a few situations species may only be available through field collection. If field collection is necessary, it is recommended that seed be collected and then the species propagated in a nursery instead of collecting entire plants. If taking plants is the only possible source of wetland plant material, precautions must be taken such as insuring that the site from which the plants are removed is not impacted to the degree that it cannot recover within a reasonable amount of time. Regulations vary on the removal of wetland plants and permits may be necessary. Factors such as collection method, timing, and storage must also be addressed.

Community types, national distribution, and shade tolerance of each species are described under **Habitat**. Types of wetland and terrestrial systems in which a species is most commonly found are listed under **Community**. Many wetland woody species, as well as transitional herbaceous species, grow in both upland and wetland communities.

The national **distribution** of each species is given because, although most of the plants in the guide do grow throughout the northeastern United States, a few do not extend entirely into the northern region. Other species may extend well outside the northeastern United States. In most cases the states or provinces given represent the limits of the species' range.

It is possible that within the ranges of the species, varieties occur. When this is known to be true, it is stated. This does not necessarily mean that the varieties are limited to certain areas or conditions. It has been determined that one species, *Spartina alterniflora*, has two ecotypes within the northeast (Garbisch personal communication). This limits the area from which plant material can be obtained (see Plant Sheet for more information). Sufficient study has not been completed on other species in the northeast which may exhibit this characteristic.

Shade tolerance is given so that the designer may determine where a particular species may be planted or what kinds of vegetation may be planted around it. Plants which are described as "tolerating" shade will also tolerate full sun unless otherwise stated (e.g., prefers full shade).

The **Notes** section contains miscellaneous information about each plant. Information was included, when available, for characteristics such as: pH preferences; beneficial qualities (e.g., soil stabilization, nitrogen fixation); susceptibility to disease, insect and wind/ice damage (mostly from Hightshoe 1988); substrate preferences; drought tolerance; etc.

When trees and shrubs are described as having male and female flowers on separate plants (dioecious) it should be recognized that in order for pollination to take place (so that fruit production may occur) both plants with male flowers and plants with female flowers should be planted (within reasonably close proximity).

Appearance

This section contains information on the general appearance of the plant such as maximum height, flower color or description, and fruit color. For trees and shrubs, maximum aerial spread is given so that spacing of the species may be determined. Other information such as flowering and fruiting period is also given. These factors are useful for aesthetic planning as well as determining wildlife use.

Wildlife Benefits

This section gives information, if available, on animals which use the plant and how they benefit from it. This is useful if one of the objectives of a wetland project is to benefit certain wildlife.

Some of the Plant Sheets may contain little or no Wildlife Benefits information. This is not necessarily because no animal uses that species, but rather that this information is not available. If the species is known to be of little use to animals, then this is stated.

The information in this section can be used not only to decide on plants which will benefit certain animals, but also to determine which animals may present a potential problem regarding depradation of planting sites. For example, woody species which are favored by deer should be protected in areas where deer populations are high.

Some species are known **not** to be used by animals which may ordinarily decimate wetland planting sites (e.g., muskrat, geese, carp). Where this is known, it is stated here. This may be useful if an animal is known to be a problem at the wetland planting site. For example, if a large population of muskrat or geese is present, *Peltandra virginica*, which is not used by these animals, may be planted to overcome the problem of eat outs.

Hydrology

Hydrology is one of the most critical aspects of wetland design. Water regime is one of the most important determining factors for which plant species will survive in an area.

Regional indicators of plants are designated by a Regional Interagency Review Panel for the U.S. Fish and Wildlife Service for use in the identification of wetlands. The **indicator status** (from Region 1, Reed 1988) for each species has been included because regulatory agencies may require the use of species with a particular status or agencies may require this information on plans and specifications. Indicator status is **not** an indication of the depth or duration of flooding that a plant will tolerate (although it is often mistaken as such). Indicators show "the estimated probability (likelihood) of a species occurring in wetlands versus nonwetlands" (Reed 1988). Reed (1988) defines the indicator categories as follows:

- **Obligate Wetland:** Occur almost always (estimated probability > 99%) under natural conditions in wetlands.

- **Facultative Wetland:** Usually occur in wetlands (estimated probability 67% - 99%), but occasionally found in nonwetlands.

- **Facultative:** Equally likely to occur in wetlands or nonwetlands (estimated probability 34% - 66%).

- **Facultative Upland:** Usually occur in nonwetlands (estimated probability 67% - 99%), but occasionally found in wetlands (estimated probability 1% - 33%).

If the given indicator status is **Facultative wetland +**, then the species is more frequently found in wetlands. **Facultative wetland –** means the species is less often found in wetlands.

Reed (1988) warns, "The wetland Indicator categories should not be equated to degrees of wetness. Many obligate wetland species occur in permanently or semipermanently flooded wetlands, but a number of obligates also occur and some are restricted to wetlands which are only temporarily or seasonally flooded."

Salinity is included in this section because it is associated with hydrology and is another extremely important factor in determining where plants survive. Species identified as living in fresh water do not tolerate any degree of salinity. **Resistant** identifies those species (mostly woody) which will occasionally tolerate conditions that may subject the plant to salt during the growing and/or dormant season (this designation does **not** describe the water tolerance of the species; refer to **Tidal Zone** and **Nontidal Regime** for information on preferred hydrology). The resistant designation was included mostly for projects which are near urban areas where salting of roads is necessary during winter months. These plants have shown more resistance to these conditions than other woody species (Hightshoe 1988). The designer should note that salting of roads usually takes place during the dormant months and that this information should not be extrapolated to mean that these plants will necessarily survive in coastal areas which occasionally undergo brackish or salty conditions (i.e., spray or flooding) during the growing season.

For species which do tolerate brackish or salt water flooding, where it is known, the maximum tolerable amount of salt in parts per thousand (ppt) are given. There are very few species for which maximum salt tolerance has been studied in detail. Some species will tolerate higher salt levels, but only for a short time. Brackish water is generally thought of as being between 1 and 15 ppt; however, not all species which tolerate brackish water will survive in water of 15 ppt. If maximum salt tolerance is not given, observing the species locally and measuring the water salinities during dry and wet seasons may be helpful in determining what salinity is acceptable for desired plants.

If the species grows in tidal areas, and the relative elevations of the area in which it typically grows are known, **tidal zone** information is provided. The tidal range can generally be divided into three zones: above mean high water (supratidal zone), from mean high water to mean low water (intertidal zone) and

below mean low water (subtidal zone). The area above mean high water can further be divided into the area above the mean spring high tide and the area between the mean spring high tide and mean high water. **Spring high tide** (spring tide) is the elevation to which the tide rises during the two times of the month when the sun, moon, and earth are in direct line with each other (during the full and new moon); at these times, tides are higher and lower than average (spring high tide has no correlation with the season of Spring). In salt marshes some species will grow only between high tide and spring high tide (e.g., *Distichlis spicata*).

Plants have extremely strict tolerances in relation to these zones. Tidal zone descriptions are based on these tolerances. Many species tolerate water levels in only a portion of each zone and some overlap into more than one, but generally these zones may be used as guides. While preferred tidal zones are given for most species, these are generalized approximations. Local populations may vary from the ranges given. For plants known to grow in tidal areas, biological references, as described below, can be helpful in the planning process, particularly if tidal zone is not stated, here. The designer can then verify or establish the preferred elevations without obtaining detailed tidal data.

Very reliable information can be found by locating a population of plants which is the same as the one which is to be established at the planting site. Species should be planted at the same elevations as those growing at the "reference site." As long as the reference site uses the same hydrology and is reasonably close to the planting site, water levels for these elevations at the sites will be identical. When working in brackish or salt water areas, salinity of the two sites should also be identical if the same vegetation is expected to survive at the planting site. Factors other than hydrology, such as soil texture, reflectance (of light), and chemistry may influence which species will survive (Bartoldus and Heliotis 1989). Selecting a reference site which is similar in every regard will insure that the same species will survive at the planting site.

Few plants will grow throughout the entire **intertidal zone**. Intertidal plants have been described as occupying a percentage of the intertidal zone. For example, *Lobelia cardinalis* is described as preferring the upper 10% of the intertidal zone. If low tide were at 0 feet and high tide were at 10 feet, *L. cardinalis* should be planted between the elevations of 9 and 10 feet. The upper 50% of the intertidal zone is from mid-tide to high tide elevation.

Most plants which grow below mean low water are submerged or floating aquatic vegetation (SAV or FAV). The depth to which submerged aquatic vegetation will grow is usually dependent on the turbidity of the water. SAV which tolerate some turbidity usually grow to lower elevations. Turbidity tolerance is given in the **Notes** section.

For plants known to grow in nontidal areas and where information was available, a **nontidal regime** is described. In nontidal areas, both flooding depth and duration determine whether a species will survive. Generally, the four regimes describing duration of flooding are defined as follows (modified from Environmental Laboratory 1987):

- **Semipermanently to permanently:** tolerates inundation or saturation from 76 - 100% of the growing season

- **Regularly:** tolerates inundation or saturation from 26 - 75% of the growing season

- **Seasonally:** tolerates inundation or saturation from 13 - 25% of the growing season

- **Irregularly:** tolerates inundation or saturation from 5 - 12% of the growing season

It is important to note that the duration given describes the percentage of the **growing season** in which the species can tolerate flooding. Plants may tolerate **saturation** which is flooding only to the surface of the soil and/or **inundation** which is flooding above the surface of the soil. Some species may require inundation (e.g., SAV or FAV) or prefer only saturation (e.g., *Symplocarpus foetidus*, most ferns). Most herbaceous emergents which tolerate some depth of inundation will also grow well under saturated conditions.

Duration of flooding that a plant may tolerate is given first, followed by whether it tolerates inundation or saturation or both. If maximum depth tolerance is known, this is also stated. A clarification of the range of duration of flooding is given in parentheses. This estimate applies to saturation and inundation. Although the estimate is given quantitatively, it should be interpreted qualitatively. The percentages given are approximations. It is usually best to verify these tolerances by finding a wetland near the planting site and determining the hydrology in which the same species which will be planted are growing.

Where maximum depth of inundation which a species may tolerate is known, this is stated. This factor is most important for herbaceous emergent plants. It is important to realize that depth tolerances are for mature plants or for plants that will break dormancy under these conditions. Species that tolerate over one foot of inundation may develop morphological adaptations (typically leaf and stem elongation) to deep water. If these species break dormancy and grow in dry or shallow water conditions, they may not develop the necessary adaptations. Plants should be grown in conditions similar to those in which they will be planted or should be planted when in a dormant state so that they will develop the proper morphology to survive (Garbisch personal communication).

Once the seeds of most woody species have germinated and as long as leaves are above the surface of the water, depth of inundation is not a limiting factor. Duration of flooding is much more important. Many of the woody species in this guide are described as tolerating seasonal or regular inundation. For most woody species, the best results under these conditions occur when there are periods of dry-down when some aeration of the soil occurs. Even species which tolerate permanent or semipermanent flooding (e.g., *Chamaecyparis thyoides*) usually are most healthy when an aeration period takes place (Laderman 1989). It is important to realize that these periods of dry-down also allow other, possibly invasive, species to colonize the site. The seeds of most woody species require aerated conditions in order to germinate and many, as saplings, prefer drier conditions than they may tolerate as mature trees (Broadfoot and Williston 1973 and Whitlow and Harris 1979).

Summary

This guide provides current and available information (**Characteristics, Appearance, Wildlife Benefits,** and **Hydrology**) for most of the trees, shrubs, herbaceous emergents, and submerged and floating aquatic vegetation that dominate the tidal and nontidal wetlands of the northeastern United States. It is organized to be of maximum utility to those individuals that are developing the designs (plans and specifications) for wetland construction, enhancement, and restoration projects.

It is also the intent of the publishers to offer similar wetland guides for other areas of the United States. This may include wetlands of the Southeast, Midwest, Southwest, and Northwest.

PLANT SHEETS

Submerged and Floating Aquatic Vegetation

Ceratophyllum demersum
Coontail, Hornwort

Characteristics
Free floating, submerged aquatic / Perennial

GROWTH
Rate of spread: rapid
Method of vegetative reproduction: fragmentation; stem fragments with lateral buds develop into new plants

PLANTING
Forms available: whole plant

HABITAT
Community: inland lakes
slow-flowing streams
fresh tidal areas

Distribution: Quebec to northern British Columbia, south to Florida, Texas, and California

NOTES
Absorbs nutrients in the water column
Tolerates some turbidity
When inland, prefers hard water
Currents and wave action break fragile stems which <u>increases</u> vegetative growth

DRB

Appearance
Description: many branches up to 9 ft. long; forms large masses
Flowering period: July through September

Wildlife Benefits
Potential Benefits and Species Served

Food (plants, seeds): ducks: wigeon, bufflehead, blue- and green-winged teals, gadwall, greater scaup, canvasback, goldeneye, pintail, redhead, ring- necked, ruddy, bluebill, shoveler, scoter, wood, mallard, and black; coots, geese, grebes, swans, marshbirds, shorebirds, gamebirds, muskrat

Cover: fish, shrimp

Supports insects which are food for fish

Carp resistant

Hydrology

Indicator status: Obligate wetland

Salinity: fresh water; less than 0.5 ppt

Tidal zone: below mean low water where depth averages 1 to 5 ft.

Nontidal regime: regularly to permanently inun- dated from 1 to 5 ft. (flooded for most of the growing season)

Elodea canadensis (Anacharis canadensis)
Waterweed

**CAUTION:
Possibly Invasive**

Characteristics
Rooted submerged aquatic / Perennial / Nonpersistent

GROWTH
Rate of spread: rapid; can clog waterways
Method of vegetative reproduction: rhizome

PLANTING
Suggested spacing:

For uniform cover	plant at
in 1 yr.	2 ft. OC
in 2 yrs.	4 ft. OC
in 3 yrs.	6 ft. OC

Forms available: bare root plant

HABITAT
Community: quiet ponds
bays
sloughs
sluggish streams or lakes

Distribution: Quebec to Saskatchewan and Washington, south to North Carolina, Alabama, Oklahoma, and California

NOTES
Prefers quiet, clear waters
Substrate preference: loamy soils
Absorbs excess nutrients in water column
Temperature preference = 10 - 25° C
pH preference = 6.5 - 10

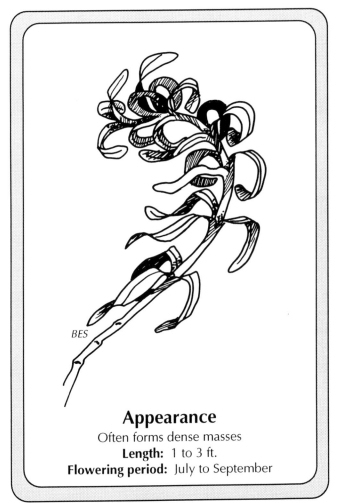

BES

Appearance
Often forms dense masses
Length: 1 to 3 ft.
Flowering period: July to September

Wildlife Benefits
Potential Benefits and Species Served

Rarely produces seed, hence, low waterfowl value

Habitat: small aquatic life

Food: beaver, waterfowl (redhead duck)

Hydrology

Indicator status: Obligate wetland

Salinity: fresh to brackish water; up to approximately 10 ppt

Tidal zone: below mean low water, depth depends on water turbidity

Nontidal regime: permanently inundated from 1 to approximately 10 ft., depth depends on water turbidity

Lemna minor
Common, Little, or Smaller duckweed

Characteristics
Unrooted floating aquatic / Perennial / Nonpersistent

GROWTH
Rate (of growth and reproduction): rapid
Method of vegetative reproduction: lateral branches
  break off to form new plants

PLANTING
Forms available: whole plant

HABITAT
Community: lakes and ponds
           slow-flowing nontidal streams
           fresh tidal waters

Distribution: Nearly world-wide

Shade: tolerates partial shade

NOTES
Aggressive because of fast reproduction
Commonly transported from other sites by waterfowl, so
  it seems to "volunteer"

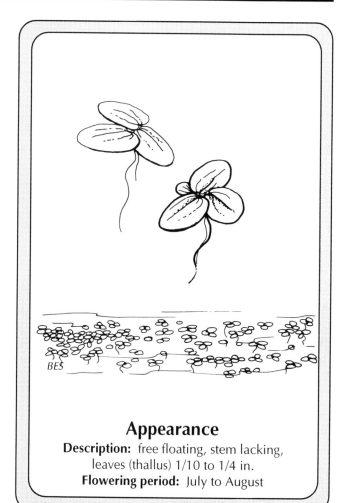

Appearance
Description: free floating, stem lacking,
  leaves (thallus) 1/10 to 1/4 in.
Flowering period: July to August

Wildlife Benefits
Potential Benefits and Species Served

Food (plants): ducks: wigeon, blue- and green-winged
  teals, mallard, wood duck; purple gallinule, coots,
  sora rail, pheasant, geese, beaver, muskrat, other
  small mammals

May be one of principal duck foods when seeds of other
  plants are not available

Hydrology

Indicator status: Obligate wetland

Salinity: fresh water; less than 0.5 ppt

Tidal zone: below mean low water (on water
  surface)

Nontidal regime: permanently inundated

Nasturtium officinale
True watercress

**CAUTION:
Possibly Invasive**

Characteristics
Rooted floating aquatic / Perennial / Nonpersistent

GROWTH
Rate of spread:
Method of vegetative reproduction: creeping stems

PLANTING
Suggested spacing:
Forms available: seed

HABITAT
Community: springs or brooks
              small ponds

Distribution: throughout the United States; varieties
   occur across its range

NOTES
Prefers areas where limestone is abundant
Introduced from Europe

BES

Appearance
Flowering period: April to October

Wildlife Benefits
Potential Benefits and Species Served

Food (sometimes available in winter): waterfowl,
   beaver, muskrat, deer

Food: attracts organisms (e.g., freshwater shrimp, water-
   bugs) which are food for trout

Cover: fish, other small aquatic life

Hydrology

Indicator status: Obligate wetland

Salinity: fresh water; less than 0.5 ppt

Tidal zone:

Nontidal regime: permanently inundated from 2 in.
   to 1 ft.

Nelumbo lutea
Lotus, Sacred bean

Characteristics
Rooted floating aquatic / Perennial / Nonpersistent

GROWTH
Rate of spread: rapid; over 1 ft. per yr. in unconsolidated sediment
Method of vegetative reproduction: rhizome

PLANTING
Suggested spacing:
Forms available: seed, tuber

HABITAT
Community: ponds (quiet water)

Distribution: New York and southern Ontario to Minnesota and Iowa, south to Florida, eastern Oklahoma and eastern Texas

Shade: tolerates partial shade

NOTES

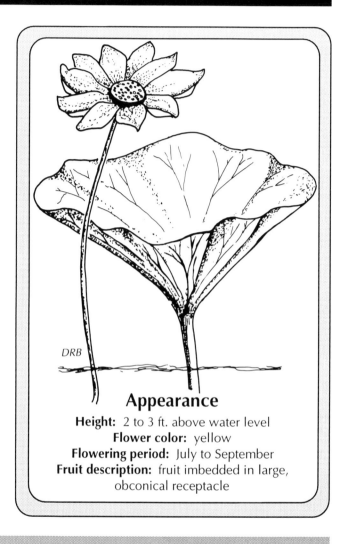

DRB

Appearance
Height: 2 to 3 ft. above water level
Flower color: yellow
Flowering period: July to September
Fruit description: fruit imbedded in large, obconical receptacle

Wildlife Benefits
Potential Benefits and Species Served

Food (seeds): waterfowl, marshbirds, songbirds

Food (rhizomes): aquatic furbearers (beaver)

Cover, Food: fish, amphibians

Hydrology

Indicator status: Obligate wetland

Salinity: fresh water; less than 0.5 ppt

Tidal zone:

Nontidal regime: permanently inundated from 1 to 5 ft.

Nymphea odorata
Fragrant water lily, Pond lily, White water lily

Characteristics
Rooted floating aquatic / Perennial / Nonpersistent

GROWTH
Rate of spread:
Method of vegetative reproduction: rhizome

PLANTING
Suggested spacing:
Forms available: bare root plant, container

HABITAT
Community: fresh tidal waters
ponds and lakes

Distribution: throughout the United States (varieties occur across this range)

Shade: tolerates partial shade

NOTES

Appearance
Height: floats on surface
Flower color: white
Flowering period: June into September

Wildlife Benefits
Potential Benefits and Species Served

Food (stems, roots, seeds): sandhill crane, redhead and canvasback ducks

Food (plants): beaver, muskrat, porcupine, moose, deer

Hydrology

Indicator status: Obligate wetland

Salinity: fresh water; less than 0.5 ppt

Tidal zone:

Nontidal regime: permanently inundated from 1 to 3 ft.

Polygonum amphibium
Water smartweed

Characteristics

Rooted, floating aquatic or erect emergent / Perennial / Nonpersistent

GROWTH
Rate of spread:
Method of vegetative reproduction: rhizome

PLANTING
Suggested spacing:
Forms available: seed, bare root plant

HABITAT
Community: nontidal waters
                fresh marshes

Distribution: Labrador and Nova Scotia to Alaska, south to Virginia, Texas, and California

Shade:

NOTES

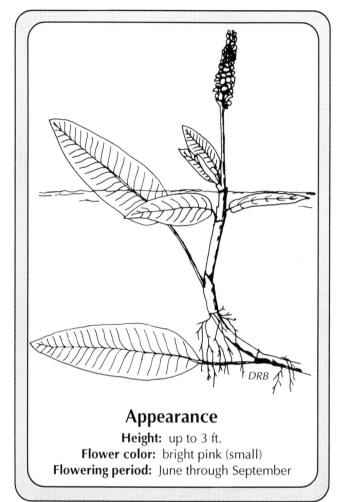

Appearance
Height: up to 3 ft.
Flower color: bright pink (small)
Flowering period: June through September

Wildlife Benefits
Potential Benefits and Species Served

Food (fruit/nutlets): waterfowl (15 duck species) and shorebirds

Food and Cover: fish

Hydrology

Indicator status: Obligate wetland

Salinity: fresh water; less than 0.5 ppt

Tidal zone:

Nontidal regime: regularly to permanently inundated up to 3 ft. or saturated (approximately 26 to 100% of the growing season)

Potamogeton nodosus *(P. americanus)*
Long-leaved pond plant

Characteristics
Rooted submerged aquatic / Perennial / Nonpersistent

GROWTH
Rate of spread: rapid; over 1 ft. per yr. in unconsolidated sediment
Method of vegetative reproduction: rhizome

PLANTING
Suggested spacing:

For uniform cover	plant at
in 1 yr.	2 ft. OC
in 2 yrs.	4 ft. OC
in 3 yrs.	6 ft. OC

Forms available: seed, bare root plant

HABITAT
Community: streams
                         lakes and ponds

Distribution: throughout the United States

NOTES
Occurs in mud or sandy soils

BES

Appearance
Stem length: up to 6 ft.
Flowering period: August to September
Flower clusters rise above water surface
(pollination by wind)

Wildlife Benefits
Potential Benefits and Species Served

Food (seeds, and/or roots): waterfowl, marshbirds, shorebirds, diving ducks, aquatic furbearers (muskrat, beaver), deer, moose

Habitat: fish

Hydrology

Indicator status: Obligate wetland

Salinity: fresh water; less than 0.5 ppt

Tidal zone:

Nontidal regime: regularly to permanently inundated at least 1 ft.; maximum depth depends on water turbidity but is usually approximately 6 ft.

Potamogeton pectinatus
Sago pond weed

Characteristics
Rooted submerged aquatic / Perennial / Nonpersistent

GROWTH
Rate of spread: rapid; over 1 ft. per yr. in unconsolidated sediment
Method of vegetative reproduction: rhizome

PLANTING
Suggested spacing:

For uniform cover	plant at
in 1 yr.	2 ft. OC
in 2 yrs.	4 ft. OC
in 3 yrs.	6 ft. OC

Forms available: seed, bare root plant

HABITAT
Community: brackish tidal waters
fresh tidal waters
lakes and ponds
streams

Distribution: Quebec and Newfoundland to Alaska and British Columbia, south to Florida, Texas and southern California

NOTES
Tolerates strong currents (but not necessarily wave action) and turbidity
Highly tolerant of eutrophic water
Prefers alkaline water; pH = 7.0 - 10.0
Grows in various substrates (e.g., silt, mud)
For more information refer to Kantrud 1990

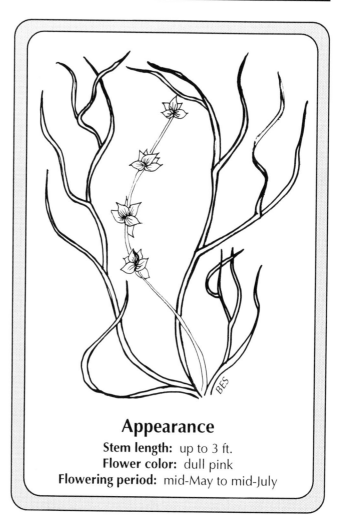

Appearance
Stem length: up to 3 ft.
Flower color: dull pink
Flowering period: mid-May to mid-July

Wildlife Benefits
Potential Benefits and Species Served

Food (seeds, rhizomes, tubers, leaves, stems): dabbling ducks, whistling (tree) ducks, and many other duck species (most important pondweed for ducks, especially diving ducks), geese, swans, long-billed dowitcher, muskrat, beaver

Food, Shelter: amphibians, reptiles, fish, and mammals

Habitat: invertebrates

Nests: coots

Hydrology

Indicator status: Obligate wetland

Salinity: fresh to moderately brackish water

Tidal zone: below mean low water; maximum depth depends on water turbidity

Nontidal regime: permanently inundated to at least 1 ft.; maximum depth depends on water turbidity and bottom texture; can be 2 to 24 ft.

Potamogeton perfoliatus
Redhead grass

Characteristics
Rooted submerged aquatic / Perennial / Nonpersistent

GROWTH
Rate of spread: rapid; over 1 ft. per yr. in unconsolidated sediment
Method of vegetative reproduction: rhizome

PLANTING
Suggested spacing:

For uniform cover	plant at
in 1 yr.	2 ft. OC
in 2 yrs.	4 ft. OC
in 3 yrs.	6 ft. OC

Forms available: seed, bare root plants

HABITAT
Community: fresh tidal waters
brackish tidal waters
ponds and streams

Distribution: Newfoundland and Quebec to Ohio, south to Florida and Louisiana (varieties occur across this range)

NOTES
Occurs in mud or sandy soil
Withstands only slow-moving water
Prefers alkaline water

Appearance
Stems: slender, short, branched
Flowering period: summer

Wildlife Benefits
Potential Benefits and Species Served

Food (seed, stems, rootstocks): ducks: redhead, canvasback, mallard, ring-necked, black; Canada goose, tundra swan

Hydrology

Indicator status: Obligate wetland

Salinity: fresh to moderately brackish water; up to approximately 5 ppt

Tidal zone: below mean low water; depth depends on water turbidity

Nontidal regime: permanently inundated to at least 1 ft.; maximum depth depends on water quality, but is usually approximately 6 ft.

Ruppia maritima
Widgeongrass, Ditch grass

Characteristics
Rooted submerged aquatic / Perennial / Nonpersistent

GROWTH
Rate of spread: rapid; over 1 ft. per yr. in unconsolidated sediment

Method of vegetative reproduction: creeping rhizome

PLANTING
Suggested spacing:

For uniform cover	plant at
in 1 yr.	2 ft. OC
in 2 yrs.	4 ft. OC
in 3 yrs.	6 ft. OC

Forms available:

HABITAT
Community: tidal salt or brackish waters

Distribution: throughout the United States (varieties occur across this range)

NOTES
Wide salinity tolerance
Tolerates some turbidity
Temperature tolerance = 7 – 35 °C
Prefers sandy substrates and shallow, calm waters

Appearance
Stem length: up to 2.5 ft.
Fruiting period: July to October

Wildlife Benefits
Potential Benefits and Species Served

High food value for waterfowl

Food (rhizomes): waterfowl, marshbirds, shorebirds, fish, invertebrates

Shelter and Nursery: fish, invertebrates

Hydrology

Indicator status: Obligate wetland

Salinity: prefers brackish to salt water (5-20 ppt); can occur in areas which often approach salinity of full sea water

Tidal zone: below mean low water; maximum depth depends on water turbidity

Nontidal regime: permanently inundated at least 1 ft.; maximum depth depends on water turbidity

Spirodela polyrhiza
Big duckweed, Water flaxseed

Characteristics
Free-floating aquatic / Perennial / Nonpersistent

GROWTH
Rate of spread: rapid
Method of vegetative reproduction: lateral branches
   break off to form new plants

PLANTING
Suggested spacing:
Forms available: whole plant

HABITAT
Community: low-current tidal waters
                slow-flowing streams
                lakes and ponds

Distribution: southeastern Quebec and southern
   Ontario to southern British Columbia, south to
   Florida, Texas, and Mexico

Shade: tolerates partial shade

NOTES
Easily dispersed by water currents and on feet of birds

BES

Appearance
Leaf length: 1/10 to 2/5 in.
Flowers: in pouches, rarely seen
Flowering period: all summer

Wildlife Benefits
Potential Benefits and Species Served

Food (plants): ducks: wigeon, blue- and green-winged
   teals, mallard, wood duck; many other waterfowl,
   purple gallinule, coots, sora rail, pheasant, beaver

Hydrology

Indicator status: Obligate wetland

Salinity: fresh water; less than 0.5 ppt

Tidal zone: below mean low water (once placed on
   surface, plant will be moved about by tide)

Nontidal regime: permanently flooded

Vallisneria americana
Wild celery, Tapegrass, Freshwater eelgrass

Characteristics
Rooted submerged aquatic / Perennial / Nonpersistent

GROWTH
Rate of spread: rapid; over 1 ft. per yr. in unconsolidated sediment
Method of vegetative reproduction: rhizome

PLANTING
Suggested spacing:

For uniform cover	plant plugs at
in 1 yr.	2 ft. OC
in 2 yrs.	4 ft. OC
in 3 yrs.	6 ft. OC

Forms available: bare root plant

HABITAT
Community: fresh to brackish tidal waters
nontidal waters

Distribution: southern New Brunswick to North Dakota, south to Florida and Texas

NOTES
Tolerates some turbidity and high nutrient load
Prefers coarse silt to slightly sandy soil
Stems root freely at joints
For more information refer to Korschgen and Green 1988

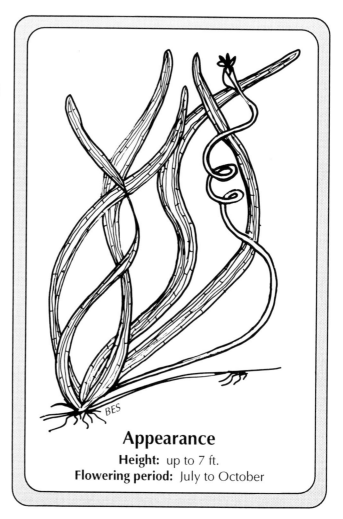

BES

Appearance
Height: up to 7 ft.
Flowering period: July to October

Wildlife Benefits
Potential Benefits and Species Served

Food (leaves, fruits): ducks: canvasback, wigeon, mallard, redhead, lesser scaup; swans, muskrat

Shade, Shelter, Supports insects, Food: fish, aquatic invertebrates

Hydrology

Indicator status: Obligate wetland

Salinity: fresh to moderately brackish water (up to approximately 5 ppt)

Tidal zone: below mean low water; depth depends on water turbidity

Nontidal regime: permanently inundated to at least 1 ft.; maximum depth depends on water turbidity

Zostera marina
Eelgrass

Characteristics
Rooted suberged aquatic / Perennial

GROWTH
Rate of spread: moderate; approximately 0.5 ft. per yr.
   in unconsolidated sediment
Method of vegetative reproduction: rhizome

PLANTING
Suggested spacing:

For uniform ground cover	plant at
in 1 yr.	1 ft. OC
in 2 yrs.	2 ft. OC
in 3 yrs.	3 ft. OC

Forms available:

HABITAT
Community: tidal salt waters (sometimes brackish)

Distribution: East Coast: Canada to North Carolina;
   West Coast: Canada to Gulf of California

NOTES
Holds nitrogen fixing bacteria in root system
Temperature range = 0 - 30° C
Grows mostly on sandy sediments
Traps sediment
Continues to grow during winter (slowly)

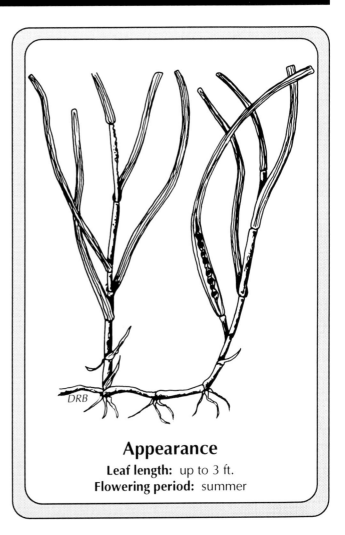

Appearance
Leaf length: up to 3 ft.
Flowering period: summer

Wildlife Benefits
Potential Benefits and Species Served

Food (rootstocks): black and American brant; ducks:
   canvasback, pintail, wigeon; beaver

Shelter, Nursery, Food: blue crab, invertebrates, fish,
   bay scallop

Important winter food (especially for brant)
Detritus attracts bacteria which is food for invertebrates

Hydrology

Indicator status: Obligate wetland

Salinity: salt water (sometimes brackish); 20 - 35 ppt

Tidal zone: below mean low water; maximum
   depth depends on water turbidity (usually where
   water is 2 - 6 ft. deep)

Nontidal regime:

PLANT SHEETS

Herbaceous Emergent Vegetation

Acorus calamus
Sweet flag, Sweet myrtle, Sea sedge

Characteristics
Herbaceous / Perennial / Nonpersistent

GROWTH
Rate of spread: moderate; approximately 0.5 ft. per yr. in unconsolidated sediment
Method of vegetative reproduction: rhizome

PLANTING
Suggested spacing:

For uniform ground cover	plant at
in 1 yr.	1 ft. OC
in 2 yrs.	2 ft. OC
in 3 yrs.	3 ft. OC

Forms available: dormant rhizome, bareroot plant, peat pot

HABITAT
Community: fresh to brackish tidal marshes
nontidal marshes
wet meadows
shallow waters

Distribution: Nova Scotia and Quebec to Montana, Oregon, and Alberta, south to Florida, Texas, and Colorado

Shade: tolerates partial shade

NOTES
Soil stabilizer
Tolerates acidic conditions

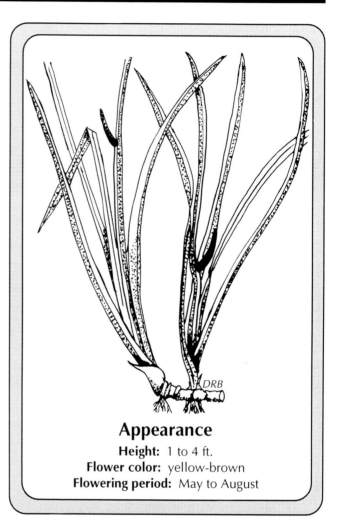

Appearance
Height: 1 to 4 ft.
Flower color: yellow-brown
Flowering period: May to August

Wildlife Benefits
Potential Benefits and Species Served

Food (rhizomes) and Cover: many species of waterfowl, muskrat

Hydrology

Indicator status: Obligate wetland

Salinity: fresh to brackish water; up to approximately 10 ppt

Tidal zone: from mean high water to spring tide elevation

Nontidal regime: regularly to permanently inundated up to 0.5 ft. or saturated (approximately 25 to 100% of the growing season)

Agrostis alba (*A. stolonifera*)
Redtop

Characteristics
Herbaceous / Perennial / Semi-persistent

GROWTH
Rate of spread: moderate
Method of vegetative reproduction: stolons

PLANTING
Suggested rate of seeding: 5 lbs. pure live seed per acre
(when seeding *A. alba* alone)
Forms available: seed

HABITAT
Community: damp thickets and swales

Distribution: Newfoundland to Yukon Territory, south
to Georgia, Louisiana, New Mexico, Arizona, and
California (varieties occur across this range)

Shade: prefers full sun

NOTES
Nurse grass -- germinates quickly, but not highly com-
petitive
Stabilizes sediment while other slower growing species
become established
Transitional area grass
Tolerates drought

Appearance
Height: up to 4 ft.
Inflorescence color: purplish to green
Flowering period: June through September

Wildlife Benefits
Potential Benefits and Species Served

Food: cottontail rabbits, some birds

Hydrology

Indicator status: Facultative wetland

Salinity: fresh water; less than 0.5 ppt

Tidal zone: above spring tide elevation

Nontidal regime: irregularly to seasonally inundated
or saturated (up to approximately 25% of the
growing season)

Alisma plantago-aquatica (*A. subcordatum*)
Water plantain, Mud plantain

Characteristics
Herbaceous / Perennial / Nonpersistent

GROWTH
Rate of spread:
Method of vegetative reproduction:

PLANTING
Suggested spacing: in clusters at irregular intervals throughout an area planted with species which provide full cover
Forms available: rootstocks, bare root plant, container

HABITAT
Community: fresh tidal marshes
nontidal marshes
edges of ponds, lakes streams
ditches, seeps
Distribution: Nova Scotia and Quebec to British Columbia, south to Florida, Texas, and Mexico
Shade:

NOTES
Grows well from seed (in shallow quiet water)

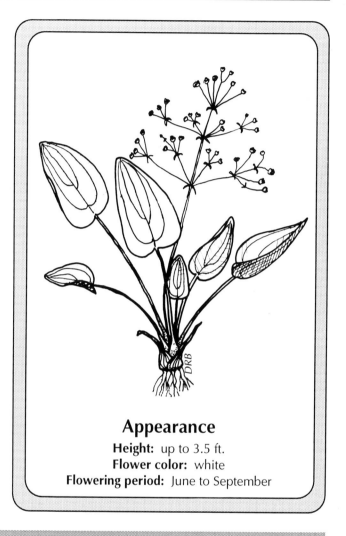

Appearance
Height: up to 3.5 ft.
Flower color: white
Flowering period: June to September

Wildlife Benefits
Potential Benefits and Species Served

Food (nutlets): waterfowl, pheasant

Hydrology
Indicator status: Obligate wetland

Salinity: fresh water; less than 0.5 ppt

Tidal zone:

Nontidal regime: regularly to permanently inundated up to 1 ft. or saturated (approximately 26 to 100% of the growing season)

Andropogon glomeratus
Lowland broom sedge, Bushy beardgrass

Characteristics
Herbaceous / Perennial / Persistent

GROWTH
Rate of spread: slow; less than 0.2 ft. per yr. in uncon-
solidated sediment; forms bunches
Method of vegetative reproduction:

PLANTING
Suggested spacing:

For uniform aerial cover	plant at
in 1 yr.	0.5 ft. OC
in 2 yrs.	1.0 ft. OC
in 3 yrs.	1.5 ft. OC

Forms available: seed, container

HABITAT
Community: freshwater marshes
wet soils
coastal areas
Distribution: Maine to Ohio, south to Florida and Texas
Shade:

NOTES
Tolerates drought
Grows in tufts

Appearance
Height: up to 5 ft.
Inflorescence color: reddish brown
Flowering period: August to October

Wildlife Benefits (*Andropogon spp.*)
Potential Benefits and Species Served

Food (seeds): finch, junco, field and tree sparrows

Food (plants): white-tailed deer

Hydrology

Indicator status: Facultative wetland +

Salinity: fresh water; less than 0.5 ppt

Tidal zone:

Nontidal regime: irregularly to seasonally inundated
or saturated (up to approximately 25% of the
growing season)

Andropogon virginicus
Broom sedge

Characteristics
Herbaceous / Perennial / Persistent

GROWTH
Rate of spread: slow; less than 0.2 ft. per yr. in unconsolidated sediment, forms bunches
Method of vegetative reproduction:

PLANTING
Suggested spacing:

For uniform aerial cover	plant at
in 1 yr.	0.5 ft. OC
in 2 yrs.	1.0 ft. OC
in 3 yrs.	1.5 ft. OC

Forms available: seed, peat pot, container

HABITAT
Community: wet meadows
transitional areas

Distribution: Massachusetts and New York to Ohio, Indiana, southern Illinois, Missouri, Kansas, south to Florida and Texas

Shade: requires full sun

NOTES
Transitional (buffer) plant
Tolerates drought
Grows in tufts

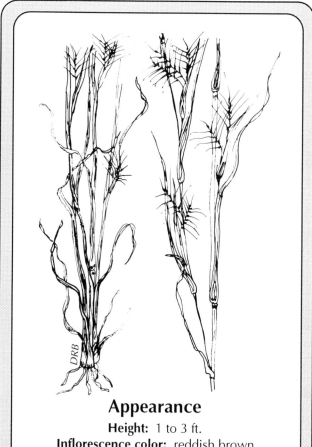

Appearance
Height: 1 to 3 ft.
Inflorescence color: reddish brown
Flowering period: August to November

Wildlife Benefits (*Andropogon spp.*)
Potential Benefits and Species Served

Food (seeds): finch, junco, field and tree sparrow

Food (plants): white-tailed deer

Cover: bobwhite

Hydrology

Indicator status: not listed

Salinity: fresh water; less than 0.5 ppt

Tidal zone:

Nontidal regime: irregularly inundated or saturated (up to approximately 12% of the growing season)

Arisaema triphyllum
Small Jack in the pulpit

Characteristics
Herbaceous / Perennial / Nonpersistent

GROWTH
Rate of spread: slow; less than 0.2 ft. per yr. in unconsolidated sediment
Method of vegetative reproduction: bulb

PLANTING
Suggested spacing: at irregular intervals throughout an area planted with species which provide full cover
Forms available: seed, dormant bulb, container

HABITAT
Community: forested seasonal wetlands
bogs
floodplains

Distribution: Nova Scotia and New Brunswick to Minnesota, south to Florida and Texas

Shade: tolerates full shade

NOTES
Tolerates drought
Spreads rapidly from seed

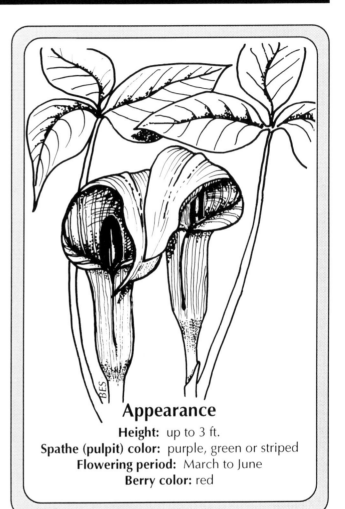

Appearance
Height: up to 3 ft.
Spathe (pulpit) color: purple, green or striped
Flowering period: March to June
Berry color: red

Wildlife Benefits
Potential Benefits and Species Served

Food (fruit, leaves): upland gamebirds (e.g., ring-necked pheasant, wild turkey), wood thrush

Hydrology

Indicator status: Facultative wetland --

Salinity: fresh water; less than 0.5 ppt

Tidal zone:

Nontidal regime: irregularly to seasonally inundated or saturated (up to approximately 25% of growing season)

Asclepias incarnata
Swamp milkweed

Characteristics
Herbaceous / Perennial / Nonpersistent

GROWTH
Rate of spread: slow; less than 0.2 ft. per yr. in unconsolidated sediment
Method of vegetative reproduction: rhizome

PLANTING
Suggested spacing: in clusters at irregular intervals throughout an area planted with species which provide full cover
Forms available: seed, rhizome, container

HABITAT
Community: fresh tidal marshes
nontidal marshes
wet meadows
shrub swamps
forested wetlands (clearings)
shores and ditches

Distribution: Nova Scotia to Manitoba and Utah, south to Florida, Louisiana, and New Mexico (varieties occur across this range)

Shade: tolerates partial shade

NOTES
Tolerates drought

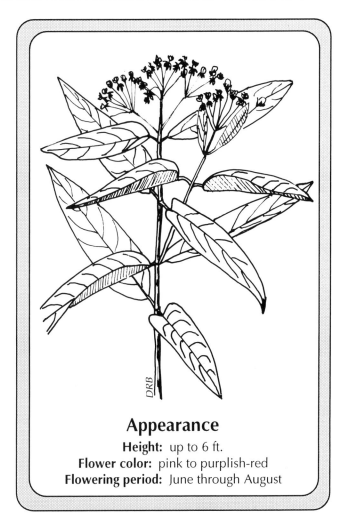

Appearance
Height: up to 6 ft.
Flower color: pink to purplish-red
Flowering period: June through August

Wildlife Benefits
Potential Benefits and Species Served

Food (roots): muskrat (sparingly)

Food (nectar): butterflies

Hydrology

Indicator status: Obligate wetland

Salinity: fresh water; less than 0.5 ppt

Tidal zone: above mean high water to spring tide elevation

Nontidal regime: irregularly, seasonally, or regularly inundated or saturated (up to approximately 75% of the growing season); when flooding is regular, only ground saturation is tolerated

Aster novae-angliae
New England aster

Characteristics
Herbaceous / Perennial / Semi-persistent

GROWTH
Rate of spread: slow; less than 0.2 ft. per yr. in unconsolidated sediment
Method of vegetative reproduction: rhizome

PLANTING
Suggested spacing: in clusters at irregular intervals throughout an area planted with species which provide full cover
Forms available: seed, live plant

HABITAT
Community: open, forested seasonal wetlands moist soils and shores

Distribution: southwestern Quebec to southern Alberta, south to central Maine, Delaware, Maryland, North Carolina, Alabama, Mississippi, Arizona, Oklahoma, Kansas, and Colorado

Shade: tolerates partial shade

NOTES
Tolerates drought

Appearance
Height: 1 to 6 ft.
Flower color: reddish purple
Flowering period: August to October

Wildlife Benefits
Potential Benefits and Species Served

Cover: many small wild game animals

Hydrology

Indicator status: Facultative wetland –

Salinity: fresh water; less than 0.5 ppt

Tidal Zone:

Nontidal regime: irregularly to seasonally inundated or saturated (up to approximately 25% of the growing season)

Atriplex patula
Orache, Marsh orache, Fat hen, Spearscale

Characteristics
Herbaceous / Annual / Nonpersistent

GROWTH
Rate of spread:
Method of vegetative reproduction: none

PLANTING
Suggested spacing: in clusters at irregular intervals throughout an area planted with species which provide full cover
Forms available: seed

HABITAT
Community: salt and brackish tidal marshes
inland saline or alkaline soils and
waste places
Distribution: Newfoundland to British Columbia, south to Nova Scotia, South Carolina, Missouri, and California (varieties occur across this range)
Shade: requires full sun

NOTES

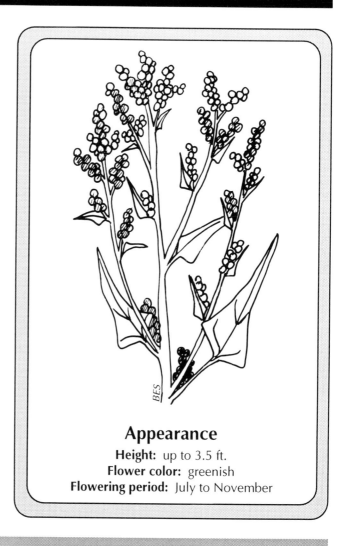

Appearance
Height: up to 3.5 ft.
Flower color: greenish
Flowering period: July to November

Wildlife Benefits
Potential Benefits and Species Served

(information not available)

Hydrology

Indicator status: Facultative wetland

Salinity: brackish to salt water

Tidal zone: above mean high water to upland

Nontidal regime:

Calamagrostis canadensis
Reed grass, Blue joint grass

Characteristics

Herbaceous / Perennial / Persistent

GROWTH

Rate of spread: slow; less than 0.2 ft. per yr. in unconsolidated sediment

Method of vegetative reproduction: rhizome

PLANTING

Suggested spacing:

For uniform aerial cover	plant at
in 1 yr.	0.5 ft. OC
in 2 yrs.	1.0 ft. OC
in 3 yrs.	1.5 ft. OC

Forms available: seed, rhizome, plug

HABITAT

Community: fresh tidal marshes
nontidal marshes
shrub swamps
wet meadows

Distribution: Newfoundland to Mackenzie and British Columbia, south to Delaware, Pennsylvania, West Virginia, northern Ohio, northern Indiana, Illinois, Missouri, Nebraska, New Mexico, and California

Shade:

NOTES

Soil stabilizer
Forms clumps

Appearance

Height: up to 5 ft.
Flowering period: June through August

Wildlife Benefits

Potential Benefits and Species Served

Food, Cover, Nesting

Grazing: mammals, especially rodents (muskrat)

Food (sprouts): moose, deer

Hydrology

Indicator status: Facultative wetland +

Salinity: fresh water; less than 0.5 ppt

Tidal zone:

Nontidal regime: seasonally to regularly inundated up to 0.5 ft. or saturated (approximately 13 to 75% of the growing season)

Caltha palustris
Marsh marigold, Cowslip, King-cup

Characteristics
Herbaceous / Perennial / Nonpersistent

GROWTH
Rate of spread: slow; less than 0.2 ft. per yr. in unconsolidated sediment
Method of vegetative reproduction: rhizome

PLANTING
Suggested spacing: in small clusters at irregular intervals throughout an area planted with species which provide full cover
Forms available: seed, bare root plant, container

HABITAT
Community: forested wetlands
shrub swamps
stream banks
seeps
wet meadows

Distribution: Labrador to Alaska, south to Newfoundland, Nova Scotia, South Carolina, Tennessee, Iowa, and Nebraska

Shade: tolerates partial shade

NOTES
Forms clumps

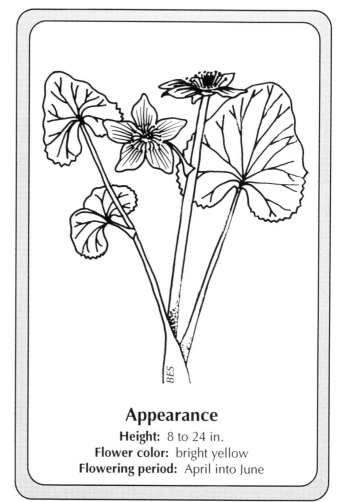

Appearance
Height: 8 to 24 in.
Flower color: bright yellow
Flowering period: April into June

Wildlife Benefits
Potential Benefits and Species Served

Food (seeds): upland game birds

Food (plants): moose

Hydrology

Indicator status: Obligate wetland

Salinity: fresh water; less than 0.5 ppt

Tidal zone:

Nontidal regime: seasonally, regularly, or permanently inundated up to 0.5 ft. (except in permanently flooded areas where water level should drop to ground surface at some time) or saturated (approximately 13 to 100% of the growing season)

Carex comosa
Bottlebrush sedge

Characteristics
Herbaceous / Perennial / Nonpersistent

GROWTH
Rate of spread: slow; less than 0.2 ft. per yr. in unconsolidated sediment
Method of vegetative reproduction: rhizome

PLANTING
Suggested spacing:

For uniform aerial cover	plant at
in 1 yr.	0.5 ft. OC
in 2 yrs.	1.0 ft. OC
in 3 yrs.	1.5 ft. OC

Forms available: seed

HABITAT
Community: wet meadow
swamps
pond edges
Distribution: western Nova Scotia, central Maine, southwestern Quebec, southern Ontario, Michigan, Wisconsin, Minnesota and Nebraska, south to Florida and Louisiana; Idaho and Washington, south to California
Shade: tolerates partial shade

NOTES

Appearance
Height: 1.5 to 4.5 ft.
Flowering period: June to August

Wildlife Benefits (*Carex spp.*)
Potential Benefits and Species Served

Food: sora and yellow rails; swamp, tree, and Lincoln sparrows; grouse, snipe, seed eating songbirds, snow bunting, larkspurs, redpoll, ruffed grouse chicks, black duck, moose

Cover

Hydrology

Indicator status: Obligate wetland

Salinity: fresh water; less than 0.5 ppt

Tidal zone:

Nontidal regime: seasonally, regularly, or permanently inundated up to 0.5 ft. or saturated (approximately 13 to 100% of the growing season); prefers fluctuating water level

Carex hystricina
Porcupine sedge

Characteristics
Herbaceous / Perennial / Nonpersistent

GROWTH
Rate of spread: moderate; approximately 0.5 ft. per yr. in unconsolidated sediment
Method of vegetative reproduction: rhizome

PLANTING
Suggested spacing:

For uniform ground cover	plant at
in 1 yr.	1 ft. OC
in 2 yrs.	2 ft. OC
in 3 yrs.	3 ft. OC

Forms available: seed, bare root plant

HABITAT
Community: wet meadows
swamps
pond shores

Distribution: Quebec to Alberta and Washington, south to New Brunswick, New England, New Jersey, District of Columbia, Tennessee, Missouri, Oklahoma, Texas, New Mexico, Arizona, and California

Shade: requires full sun

NOTES

Appearance
Height: 1 to 3 ft.
Flowering period: June to August

Wildlife Benefits (*Carex spp.*)
Potential Benefits and Species Served

Food: sora and yellow rails; swamp, tree, and Lincoln sparrows; grouse, snipe, seed eating songbirds, snow bunting, larkspurs, redpoll, ruffed grouse chicks, black duck, moose

Cover

Hydrology

Indicator status: Obligate wetland

Salinity: fresh water; less than 0.5 ppt

Tidal zone:

Nontidal regime: seasonally, regularly, or permanently inundated up to 0.5 ft. or saturated (approximately 13 to 100% of the growing season); prefers fluctuating water level

Carex lacustris
Lake sedge, Ripgut

Characteristics
Herbaceous / Perennial / Nonpersistent

GROWTH
Rate of spread: rapid; over 1 ft. per yr. in unconsolidated sediment
Method of vegetative reproduction: rhizome

PLANTING
Suggested spacing:

For uniform ground cover	plant at
in 1 yr.	2 ft. OC
in 2 yrs.	4 ft. OC
in 3 yrs.	6 ft. OC

Forms available: seed, bare root plant, peat or fiber pot

HABITAT
Community: nontidal marshes
nontidal swamps
lake margins

Distribution: Quebec to southern Manitoba, south to Nova Scotia, New England, Virginia, Ohio, Indiana, Illinois, Iowa, South Dakota

Shade: requires full sun

NOTES

Appearance
Height: 2 to 4 ft.
Flowering period: May to August

Wildlife Benefits (*Carex spp.*)
Potential Benefits and Species Served

Food: sora and yellow rails; swamp, tree, and Lincoln sparrows; grouse, snipe, seed eating songbirds, snow bunting, larkspurs, redpoll, ruffed grouse chicks, black duck, moose

Cover

Hydrology

Indicator status: Obligate wetland

Salinity: fresh water; less than 0.5 ppt

Tidal zone:

Nontidal regime: seasonally, regularly, or permanently inundated up to 2 ft. or saturated (approximately 13 to 100% of the growing season); prefers fluctuating water level

Carex lanuginosa
Wooly sedge

Characteristics
Herbaceous / Perennial / Nonpersistent

GROWTH
Rate of spread:
Method of vegetative reproduction: rhizome

PLANTING
Suggested spacing:
Forms available: peat or fiber pot

HABITAT
Community: wet meadows
pond shores

Distribution: Quebec to British Columbia south to New Brunswick, New England, Virginia, Tennessee, Arkansas, Oklahoma, Texas, New Mexico, Arizona, and southern California

Shade:

NOTES
Robust
Streambank stabilizer
Tolerates drought

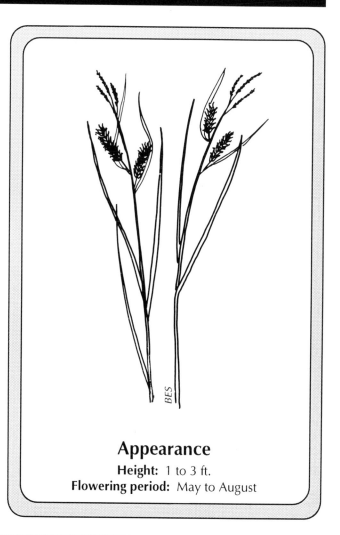

Appearance
Height: 1 to 3 ft.
Flowering period: May to August

Wildlife Benefits (*Carex spp.*)
Potential Benefits and Species Served

Food: sora and yellow rails; swamp, tree, and Lincoln sparrows; grouse, snipe, seed eating songbirds, snow bunting, larkspurs, redpoll, ruffed grouse chicks, black duck, moose

Cover

Hydrology

Indicator status: Obligate wetland

Salinity: fresh water; less than 0.5 ppt

Tidal zone:

Nontidal regime: irregularly, seasonally, or regularly inundated up to 0.5 ft. or saturated (up to approximately 75% of the growing season); prefers fluctuating water level

Carex retrorsa
Retrorse sedge

Characteristics
Herbaceous / Perennial / Nonpersistent

GROWTH
Rate: slow; less than 0.2 ft. per yr. in unconsolidated sediment
Method of vegetative reproduction: rhizome

PLANTING
Suggested spacing:

For uniform aerial cover	plant at
in 1 yr.	0.5 ft. OC
in 2 yrs.	1.0 ft. OC
in 3 yrs.	1.5 ft. OC

Forms available: seed, rhizome, bare root plant

HABITAT
Community: wet meadow
forested seasonal wetland

Distribution: Quebec to British Columbia, south to Nova Scotia, New England, northern New Jersey, Pennsylvania, northern Ohio, northern Indiana, northern Illinois, northern Iowa, South Dakota, Colorado, Utah, Washington

Shade: tolerates full shade

NOTES

Appearance
Height: 1 to 3 ft.
Flowering period: July to October

Wildlife Benefits (*Carex spp.*)
Potential Benefits and Species Served

Food: sora and yellow rails; swamp, tree, and Lincoln sparrows; grouse, snipe, seed eating songbirds, snow bunting, larkspurs, redpoll, ruffed grouse chicks, black duck, moose

Cover

Hydrology

Indicator status: Facultative wetland +

Salinity: fresh water; less than 0.5 ppt

Tidal zone:

Nontidal regime: irregularly, seasonally, regularly, or permanently inundated up to 0.5 ft. or saturated (up to 100% of the growing season); prefers fluctuating water level

Carex stipata
Awl-fruited sedge

Characteristics
Herbaceous / Perennial / Nonpersistent

GROWTH
Rate of spread: slow; less than 0.2 ft. per yr. in unconsolidated sediment
Method of vegetative reproduction: rhizome

PLANTING
Suggested spacing:

For uniform aerial cover	plant at
in 1 yr.	0.5 ft. OC
in 2 yrs.	1.0 ft. OC
in 3 yrs.	1.5 ft. OC

Forms available: seed

HABITAT
Community: nontidal marshes
    wet meadows

Distribution: southern Labrador, to southern Alaska, south to Newfoundland, Nova Scotia, New England, North Carolina, Tennessee, Missouri, Kansas, New Mexico, and California

Shade: tolerates partial shade

NOTES
Tolerates drought

Appearance
Height: 1 to 3 ft.
Flowering period: May to August

Wildlife Benefits (*Carex spp.*)
Potential Benefits and Species Served

Food: sora and yellow rails; swamp, tree, and Lincoln sparrows; grouse, snipe, seed eating songbirds, snow bunting, larkspurs, redpoll, ruffed grouse chicks, black duck, moose

Cover

Hydrology

Indicator status: Not listed

Salinity: fresh water; less than 0.5 ppt

Tidal zone:

Nontidal regime: irregularly to seasonally inundated or saturated (up to approximately 25% of the growing season)

Carex stricta
Tussock sedge, Uptight sedge

Characteristics
Herbaceous / Perennial / Semi-persistent

GROWTH
Rate of spread: moderate; approximately 0.5 ft. per yr. in unconsolidated sediment
Method of vegetative reproduction: rhizome

PLANTING
Suggested spacing:

For uniform ground cover	plant at
in 1 yr.	1 ft. OC
in 2 yrs.	2 ft. OC
in 3 yrs.	3 ft. OC

Forms available: seed, bare root plant

HABITAT
Community: fresh tidal marshes
nontidal marshes
shrub swamps
forested wetlands
wet swales

Distribution: New Brunswick to Ontario, south to Nova Scotia, New England, North Carolina, Ohio, Indiana, Illinois, Minnesota

Shade: requires full sun

NOTES
Tolerates acidic conditions
Forms clumps or "tussocks"

Appearance
Height: up to 3.5 ft.
Inflorescence: inconspicuous
Flowering period: May through August

Wildlife Benefits (*Carex spp.*)
Potential Benefits and Species Served

Food: sora and yellow rails; swamp, tree, and Lincoln sparrows; grouse, snipe, seed eating songbirds, snow bunting, larkspurs, redpoll, ruffed grouse chicks, black duck, moose

Cover

Hydrology

Indicator status: Obligate wetland

Salinity: fresh water; less than 0.5 ppt

Tidal zone: upper 10% of intertidal zone and above to spring tide elevation

Nontidal regime: seasonally, regularly, or permanently inundated up to 0.5 ft. or saturated (approximately 13 to 100% of the growing season)

Carex vulpinoidea
Fox sedge

Characteristics
Herbaceous / Perennial / Nonpersistent

GROWTH
Rate of spread: slow; less than 0.2 ft. per yr. in unconsolidated sediment

Method of vegetative reproduction: rhizome

PLANTING
Suggested spacing:

For uniform aerial cover	plant at
in 1 yr.	0.5 ft. OC
in 2 yrs.	1.0 ft. OC
in 3 yrs.	1.5 ft. OC

Forms available: seed, bare root plant, peat or fiber pot

HABITAT
Community: freshwater marshes
wet meadows

Distribution: Newfoundland to southern British Columbia, Washington, Oregon, south to Florida, west to the Rocky Mountains

Shade: tolerates partial shade

NOTES

Appearance
Height: up to 3.5 ft.
Flowering period: June through August

Wildlife Benefits (*Carex spp.*)
Potential Benefits and Species Served

Food: sora and yellow rails; swamp, tree, and Lincoln sparrows; grouse, snipe, seed eating songbirds, snow bunting, larkspurs, redpoll, ruffed grouse chicks, black duck, moose

Cover

Hydrology
Indicator status: Obligate wetland

Salinity: fresh water; less than 0.5 ppt

Tidal zone:

Nontidal regime: seasonally to regularly inundated up to 0.5 ft. or saturated (approximately 13 to 75% of the growing season); prefers fluctuating water level

Cyperus esculentus
Chufa, Ground almond, Yellow nutgrass, Yellow nutsedge

Characteristics
Herbaceous / Perennial / Nonpersistent

GROWTH
Rate of spread: rapid; over 1 ft. per yr. in unconsolidated sediment
Method of vegetative reproduction: rhizome

PLANTING
Suggested spacing: 50 pounds of tubers per acre
Forms available: seed, tuber, peat pot

HABITAT
Community: fresh tidal marshes
nontidal marshes
swamps
wet shores
wet meadows, swales

Distribution: Nova Scotia and Quebec west to Washington, south throughout the United States

Shade: requires full sun

NOTES
Dry-down initiates new stem growth from tubers
pH preference = 5.0 - 7.5
Does not tolerate drought

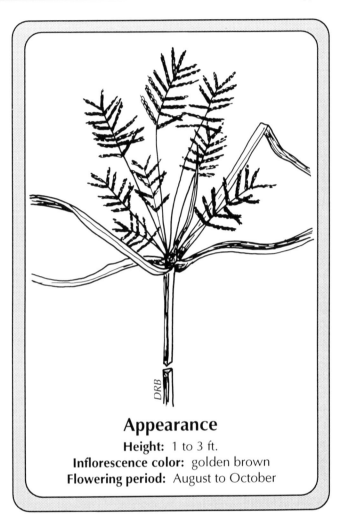

Appearance
Height: 1 to 3 ft.
Inflorescence color: golden brown
Flowering period: August to October

Wildlife Benefits
Potential Benefits and Species Served

Food (seeds, rhizomes): waterfowl, upland gamebirds, songbirds, terrestrial furbearers, small mammals

Produces edible rhizomes which are ranked as the tenth most valuable waterfowl food in the United States

Hydrology

Indicator status: Facultative wetland

Salinity: fresh water; less than 0.5 ppt

Tidal zone:

Nontidal regime: irregularly, seasonally, or regularly inundated up to 1 ft. or saturated (tolerates frequent, temporary inundation up to approximately 75% of the growing season)

Distichlis spicata
Salt grass, Spike grass, Alkali grass

Characteristics
Herbaceous / Perennial / Persistent

GROWTH
Rate of spread: moderate; approximately 0.5 ft. per yr. in unconsolidated sediment

Method of vegetative reproduction: rhizome

PLANTING
Suggested spacing:

For uniform ground cover	plant at
in 1 yr.	1 ft. OC
in 2 yrs.	2 ft. OC
in 3 yrs.	3 ft. OC

Forms available: bare root plant, peat or fiber pot

HABITAT
Community: tidal salt marshes

Distribution: New Brunswick, south to Florida and Texas, locally inland to Missouri and along Pacific coast

Shade: requires full sun

NOTES
Tolerates alkaline soils (pH range = 4.1 - 9.5)
Often found in poorly drained soil

Appearance
Height: 8 to 16 in.
Flowering period: August into October

Wildlife Benefits
Potential Benefits and Species Served

Food (seed heads, young plants, rootstocks): shoveler, teals, Canada goose

Hydrology

Indicator status: Facultative wetland +

Salinity: salt water; up to 50 ppt

Tidal zone: from mean high water to spring tide elevation

Nontidal regime:

Dulichium arundinaceum
Three-sided sedge

Characteristics
Herbaceous / Perennial / Nonpersistent

GROWTH
Rate of spread:
Method of vegetative reproduction: rhizome

PLANTING
Suggested spacing:
Forms available: bare root plant, container

HABITAT
Community: fresh tidal marshes
nontidal marshes
bogs
swamps
pond edges

Distribution: Newfoundland to British Columbia, south to Florida, Texas, and California

Shade: tolerates partial shade

NOTES
Readily transplanted by cores

Appearance
Height: up to 3.5 ft.
Flowering period: July to October

Wildlife Benefits
Potential Benefits and Species Served

Food: muskrat, wildfowl (of slight importance)

Hydrology

Indicator status: Obligate wetland

Salinity: fresh water; less than 0.5 ppt

Tidal zone:

Nontidal regime: regularly to permanently inundated up to 1 ft. (shallow water preferred) or saturated (approximately 26 to 100% of the growing season, although does better where water rarely draws down)

Eleocharis equisetoides
Knotted spike rush

Characteristics
Herbaceous / Perennial / Nonpersistent

GROWTH
Rate of spread:
Method of vegetative reproduction: rhizome

PLANTING
Suggested spacing:
Forms available: rhizome

HABITAT
Community: nontidal marshes
pond edges

Distribution: Massachusetts and New York to Michigan
and Missouri, south to central Florida and Texas

Shade:

NOTES

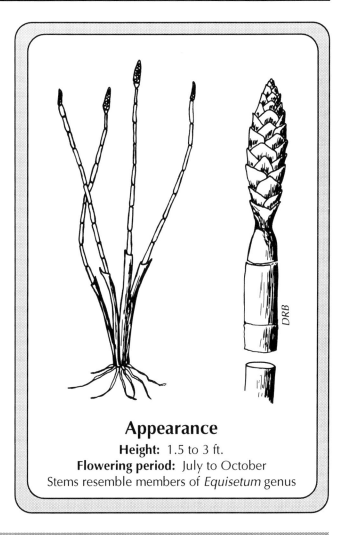

Appearance
Height: 1.5 to 3 ft.
Flowering period: July to October
Stems resemble members of *Equisetum* genus

Wildlife Benefits (*Eleocharis spp.*)
Potential Benefits and Species Served

Food (seeds, rhizomes): ducks: wigeon, black, mallard,
mottled, ring-necked, shoveler, blue- and green-
winged teals; Canada and snow geese; whistling
swan

Food (seeds): sora and Virginia rails

Food (plants): muskrat, cottontail rabbit

Hydrology

Indicator status: Obligate wetland

Salinity: fresh water; less than 0.5 ppt

Tidal zone:

Nontidal regime: regularly to permanently inundated up to 1 ft. or saturated (approximately 26
to 100% of the growing season)

Eleocharis obtusa (E. ovata)
Blunt spike rush

Characteristics
Herbaceous / Annual / Nonpersistent

GROWTH
Rate of spread:
Method of vegetative reproduction: none

PLANTING
Suggested spacing:
Forms available: bare root plant

HABITAT
Community: wet meadows

Distribution: Nova Scotia and New Brunswick to Minnesota, south to northwestern Florida, Alabama, Mississippi, Louisiana, and eastern Texas, also British Columbia to northern California, Colorado, and New Mexico

Shade: requires full sun

NOTES
Requires dry-down period in order for seed to germinate

Appearance
Height: 0.5 to 2 ft.
Flowering period: July to September

Wildlife Benefits (*Eleocharis spp.*)
Potential Benefits and Species Served

Food (seeds, rhizomes): ducks: wigeon, black, mallard, mottled, ring-necked, shoveler, blue- and green-winged teals; Canada and snow geese; whistling swan

Food (seeds): sora and Virginia rails

Food (plants): muskrat, cottontail rabbit

Hydrology

Indicator status: Obligate wetland

Salinity: fresh water; less than 0.5 ppt

Tidal zone: upper 10% of intertidal zone and above to spring tide elevation

Nontidal regime: regularly to semipermanently in-undated up to 0.5 ft. or saturated (approximately 26 to nearly 100% of the growing season)

Eleocharis palustris
Marsh spike rush

Characteristics
Herbaceous / Perennial / Nonpersistent

GROWTH
Rate of spread: moderate; approximately 0.5 ft. per yr. in unconsolidated sediment
Method of vegetative reproduction: rhizome

PLANTING
Suggested spacing:

For uniform ground cover	plant at
in 1 yr.	1 ft. OC
in 2 yrs.	2 ft. OC
in 3 yrs.	3 ft. OC

Forms available: rhizome

HABITAT
Community: fresh tidal marshes
nontidal marshes
pond and stream edges

Distribution: southern Labrador to British Columbia south to New Jersey, Pennsylvania, southern Michigan, Illinois, Iowa, South Dakota, Wyoming, and northern California (varieties occur across this range)

Shade: tolerates partial shade

NOTES
Tolerates alkaline soil

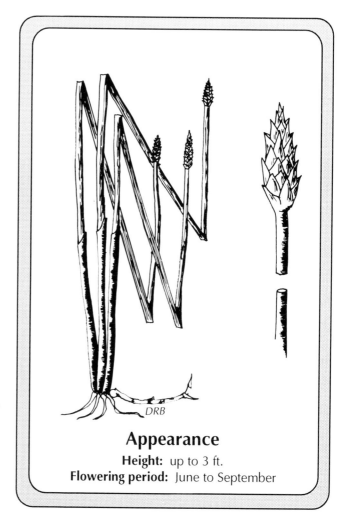

Appearance
Height: up to 3 ft.
Flowering period: June to September

Wildlife Benefits (*Eleocharis spp.*)
Potential Benefits and Species Served

Food (seeds, rhizomes): ducks: wigeon, black, mallard, mottled, ring-necked, shoveler, blue- and green-winged teals; Canada and snow geese; whistling swan

Food (seeds): sora and Virginia rails

Food (plants): muskrat, cottontail rabbit

Hydrology

Indicator status: Obligate wetland

Salinity: fresh water (possibly brackish)

Tidal zone:

Nontidal regime: seasonally, regularly, or permanently saturated (approximately 13 to 100% of the growing season)

Eleocharis quadrangulata
Square-stemmed spike rush

Characteristics
Herbaceous / Perennial / Nonpersistent

GROWTH
Rate: slow; less than 0.2 ft. per yr. in unconsolidated sediment
Method of vegetative reproduction: rhizome

PLANTING
Suggested spacing:

For uniform aerial cover	plant at
in 1 yr.	0.5 ft. OC
in 2 yrs.	1.0 ft. OC
in 3 yrs.	1.5 ft. OC

Forms available:

HABITAT
Community: fresh tidal marshes
nontidal marshes
lake and pond edges

Distribution: Massachusetts to Ontario, Michigan, Illinois, Wisconsin, and Missouri, south to Florida, Texas, and Oklahoma

Shade: prefers full sun

NOTES

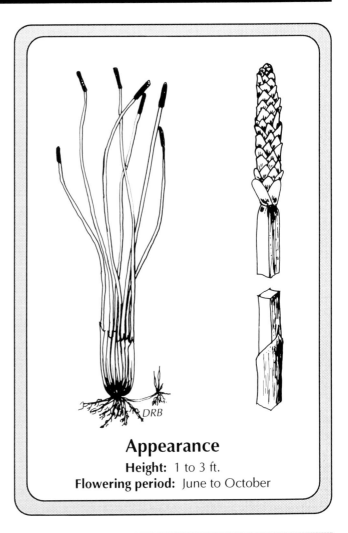

Appearance
Height: 1 to 3 ft.
Flowering period: June to October

Wildlife Benefits (*Eleocharis spp.*)
Potential Benefits and Species Served

Food (seeds, rhizomes): ducks: wigeon, black, mallard, mottled, ring-necked, shoveler, blue- and green-winged teals; Canada and snow geese; whistling swan

Food (seeds): sora and Virginia rails

Food (plants): muskrat, cottontail rabbit

Hydrology

Indicator status: Obligate wetland

Salinity: fresh water; less than 0.5 ppt

Tidal zone:

Nontidal regime: regularly to permanently inundated up to 1 ft. or saturated (approximately 26 to 100% of the growing season)

Glyceria canadensis
Rattlesnake mannagrass

Characteristics
Herbaceous / Perennial / Semipersistent

GROWTH
Rate of spread: moderate; approximately 0.5 ft. per yr. in unconsolidated sediment
Method of vegetative reproduction: rhizome

PLANTING
Suggested spacing:

For uniform ground cover	plant at
in 1 yr.	1 ft. OC
in 2 yrs.	2 ft. OC
in 3 yrs.	3 ft. OC

Forms available: seed, plug

HABITAT
Community: forested wetlands
bogs
wet meadows

Distribution: Newfoundland to Minnesota, south to New Jersey and Illinois

Shade: requires full sun

NOTES
Does not compete well with other species; should be planted as a monotypic stand

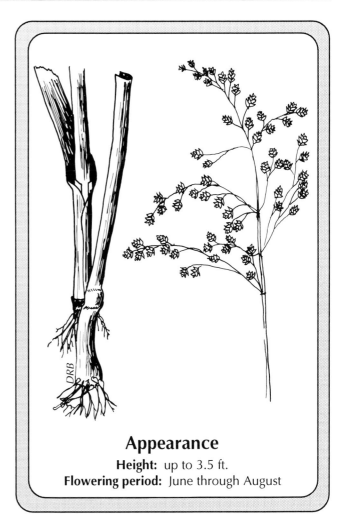

Appearance
Height: up to 3.5 ft.
Flowering period: June through August

Wildlife Benefits (*Glyceria spp.*)
Potential Benefits and Species Served

Food: waterfowl, muskrat

Browsing: deer (heavily)

Hydrology

Indicator status: Obligate wetland

Salinity: fresh water; less than 0.5 ppt

Tidal zone:

Nontidal regime: regularly inundated up to approximately 1 ft. or saturated (up to approximately 50% of the growing season)

Glyceria grandis
Reed meadow grass, American mannagrass

Characteristics
Herbaceous / Perennial / Nonpersistent

GROWTH
Rate of spread: rapid; over 1 ft. per yr. in unconsolidated sediment

Method of vegetative reproduction: primarily rhizome, also by stolon

PLANTING
Suggested spacing:

For uniform ground cover	plant at
in 1 yr.	2 ft. OC
in 2 yrs.	4 ft. OC
in 3 yrs.	6 ft. OC

Forms available: plug

HABITAT
Community: nontidal marsh

Distribution: Newfoundland to Alaska, south to Virginia, Tennessee, Iowa, New Mexico, and Oregon

Shade: requires full sun

NOTES
Does not compete well with other species; should be planted as a monotypic stand

Appearance
Height: 3 to 5 ft.
Flowering period: June to August

Wildlife Benefits (*Glyceria spp.*)
Potential Benefits and Species Served

Food: waterfowl, muskrat

Browsing: deer (heavily)

Hydrology

Indicator status: Obligate wetland

Salinity: fresh water; less than 0.5 ppt

Tidal zone:

Nontidal regime: seasonally inundated up to 1 ft. or saturated (tolerates inundation in spring but requires draw-down by late spring)

Glyceria pallida (*Puccinellia fernalidii, P. pallida*)
Floating mannagrass

Characteristics
Herbaceous / Perennial / Nonpersistent

GROWTH
Rate of spread: rapid; over 1 ft. per yr. in unconsolidated sediment

Method of vegetative reproduction: primarily by stolon, also by rhizome

PLANTING
Suggested spacing:

For uniform ground cover	plant at
in 1 yr.	2 ft. OC
in 2 yrs.	4 ft. OC
in 3 yrs.	6 ft. OC

Forms available: plug

HABITAT
Community: pond edges
               sloughs
               pools

Distribution: Nova Scotia and southern Maine to southern Ontario, south to Virginia, Tennessee, and southeastern Missouri

Shade: tolerates partial shade

NOTES
When inundated, becomes floating-stemmed aquatic

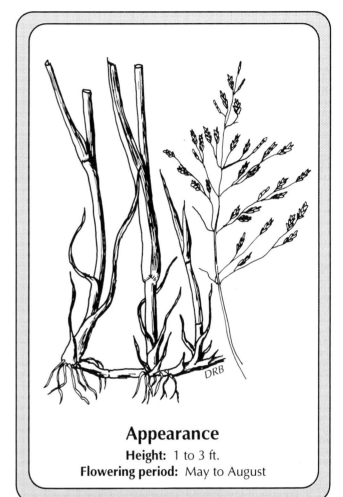

Appearance
Height: 1 to 3 ft.
Flowering period: May to August

Wildlife Benefits (*Glyceria spp.*)
Potential Benefits and Species Served

Food: waterfowl, muskrat

Browsing: deer (heavily)

Hydrology

Indicator status: Obligate wetland

Salinity: fresh water; less than 0.5 ppt

Tidal zone:

Nontidal regime: regularly to semipermanently inundated up to 1.0 ft. or saturated (approximately 25 to nearly 100% of the growing season)

Glyceria septentrionalis
Mannagrass, Floating manna, Sweet grass, Eastern mannagrass

Characteristics
Herbaceous / Perennial / Nonpersistent

GROWTH
Rate of spread: rapid; over 1 ft. per yr. in unconsolidated sediment

Method of vegetative reproduction: primarily rhizome, also by stolon

PLANTING
Suggested spacing:

For uniform ground cover	plant at
in 1 yr.	2 ft. OC
in 2 yrs.	4 ft. OC
in 3 yrs.	6 ft. OC

Forms available: plug

HABITAT
Community: nontidal marshes
pond and lake edges

Distribution: eastern Massachusetts to southern Ontario, south to Georgia, Kentucky, Missouri, and Texas

Shade: requires full sun

NOTES
Most growth takes place during spring and fall with a dormant period after blooming; good species for Autumn planting

Does not compete well with other species; should be planted as a monotypic stand

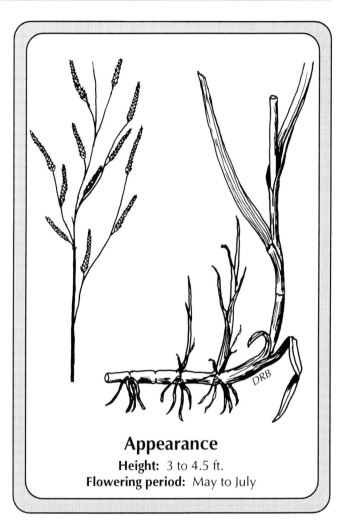

Appearance
Height: 3 to 4.5 ft.
Flowering period: May to July

Wildlife Benefits (*Glyceria spp.*)
Potential Benefits and Species Served

Food: waterfowl, muskrat

Browsing: deer (heavily)

Hydrology

Indicator status: Obligate wetland

Salinity: fresh water; less than 0.5 ppt

Tidal zone:

Nontidal regime: seasonally inundated up to 1.0 ft. or saturated (tolerates inundation in spring but requires draw down by late spring)

Glyceria striata
Fowl mannagrass, Nerved mannagrass

Characteristics
Herbaceous / Perennial / Nonpersistent

GROWTH
Rate of spread:
Method of vegetative reproduction: rhizome

PLANTING
Suggested spacing:
Forms available: seed, plug

HABITAT
Community: freshwater marshes
shrub and forested wetlands
seeps

Distribution: Newfoundland and Labrador to British Columbia, south to Florida and California

Shade: prefers partial shade, may tolerate full shade

NOTES
Grows in tussocks, intermixes with other species

Appearance
Height: up to 4 ft.
Flowering period: June into September

Wildlife Benefits (*Glyceria spp.*)
Potential Benefits and Species Served

Food: waterfowl, muskrat

Browsing: deer (heavily)

Hydrology

Indicator status: Obligate wetland

Salinity: fresh water; less than 0.5 ppt

Tidal zone:

Nontidal regime: irregularly to seasonally inundated or saturated (up to approximately 25% of the growing season)

Hibiscus moscheutos
Marsh hibiscus

Characteristics
Herbaceous / Perennial / Persistent

GROWTH
Rate of spread: slow; less than 0.2 ft. per yr. in unconsolidated sediment
Method of vegetative reproduction:

PLANTING
Suggested spacing: at irregular intervals throughout an area planted with species which provide full cover
Forms available: bare root plant, container, peat or fiber pot

HABITAT
Community: fresh to brackish tidal marshes occasionally nontidal marshes
Distribution: Massachusetts to Florida and Alabama, inland from western New York and southern Ontario to northern Illinois and Indiana
Shade: tolerates partial sun

NOTES

Appearance
Height: 3.5 to 7 ft.
Flower color: pink or white
(large and showy)
Flowering period: July through September

Wildlife Benefits
Potential Benefits and Species Served

Limited

Nectar: ruby-throated hummingbird

Hydrology

Indicator status: Obligate wetland

Salinity: fresh to brackish water; up to approximately 15 ppt

Tidal zone: upper 20% of intertidal zone and above to spring tide elevation

Nontidal regime: irregularly to regularly inundated up to 3 in. or saturated (tolerates frequent, temporary inundation up to approximately 75% of the growing season)

Hydrocotyle umbellata
Water-pennywort

Characteristics
Herbaceous / Perennial / Nonpersistent

GROWTH
Rate of spread:
Method of vegetative reproduction: stolons or rhizomes

PLANTING
Suggested spacing:
Forms available: bare root plant

HABITAT
Community: tidal marshes
shores
ditches

Distribution: Nova Scotia to Minnesota, south to Florida, Oklahoma, and Texas; Oregon and California

Shade: tolerates partial shade

NOTES

Appearance
Height: up to 1 ft.
Flower color: white
Flowering period: May to September

Wildlife Benefits
Potential Benefits and Species Served

Food (seeds, leaves): wildfowl, waterfowl

Hydrology

Indicator status: Obligate wetland

Salinity: fresh water; less than 0.5 ppt

Tidal zone:

Nontidal regime: regularly to permanently inundated up to 1 ft. or saturated (approximately 26 to 100% of the growing season)

Iris pseudacorus
Yellow water iris

Characteristics
Herbaceous / Perennial / Nonpersistent

GROWTH
Rate of spread: slow; less than 0.2 ft. per yr. in unconsolidated sediment
Method of vegetative reproduction: bulb

PLANTING
Suggested spacing:

For uniform aerial cover	plant at
in 1 yr.	0.5 ft. OC
in 2 yrs.	1.0 ft. OC
in 3 yrs.	1.5 ft. OC

Forms available: seed, dormant bulb, bare root plant, container

HABITAT
Community: fresh tidal marshes
nontidal marshes
swamps
wet meadows and shores

Distribution: Newfoundland to Minnesota, southward

Shade: requires full sun for flowers, will tolerate partial shade but will not flower

NOTES
Remains in clumps

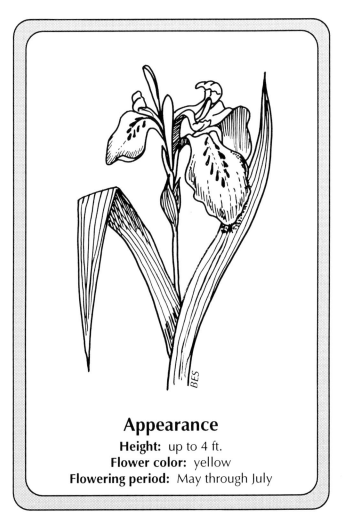

Appearance
Height: up to 4 ft.
Flower color: yellow
Flowering period: May through July

Wildlife Benefits (*Iris spp.*)
Potential Benefits and Species Served

Food: muskrat, wildfowl (probably not seeds), marsh birds (persists as cover within a growing season under heavy grazing)

Hydrology

Indicator status: Obligate wetland

Salinity: fresh water; less than 0.5 ppt

Tidal zone: near mean high water

Nontidal regime: regularly to permanently inundated up to 0.5 ft. or saturated (approximately 26 to 100% of the growing season)

Iris versicolor
Blue flag, Blue water iris, Poison flag, Clajeux

Characteristics
Herbaceous / Perennial / Nonpersistent

GROWTH
Rate of spread: slow; less than 0.2 ft. per yr. in unconsolidated sediment

Method of vegetative reproduction: bulb

PLANTING
Suggested spacing:

For uniform aerial cover	plant at
in 1 yr.	0.5 ft. OC
in 2 yrs.	1.0 ft. OC
in 3 yrs.	1.5 ft. OC

Forms available: seed, dormant bulb, bare root plant, container

HABITAT
Community: fresh to moderately brackish tidal marshes
wet meadows and shores
swamps
forested wetlands (occasionally)

Distribution: Newfoundland to Manitoba, south to Virginia and Minnesota

Shade: requires full sun for flowers, will tolerate partial shade but will not flower

NOTES
Remains in clumps
Prefers acidic soil
Severe dermatitus may result from handling rhizome

Appearance
Height: up to 4 ft.
Flower color: blue or violet
Flowering period: May through July

Wildlife Benefits (*Iris spp.*)
Potential Benefits and Species Served

Food: muskrat, wildfowl (probably not seeds), marsh birds (persists as cover within a growing season under heavy grazing)

Hydrology

Indicator status: Obligate wetland

Salinity: fresh to moderately brackish water

Tidal zone: near mean high water

Nontidal regime: regularly to permanently inundated up to 0.5 ft. or saturated (approximately 26 to 100% of the growing season)

Juncus balticus
Salt rush, Baltic rush

Characteristics
Herbaceous / Perennial

GROWTH
Rate of spread: slow; less than 0.2 ft. per yr. in unconsolidated sediment
Method of vegetative reproduction: rhizome

PLANTING
Suggested spacing:

For uniform aerial cover	plant at
in 1 yr.	0.5 ft. OC
in 2 yrs.	1.0 ft. OC
in 3 yrs.	1.5 ft. OC

Forms available: seed, rhizome

HABITAT
Community: salt and brackish tidal marshes
calcareous nontidal marshes
dunes

Distribution: Labrador and Newfoundland to British Columbia, south to Pennsylvania and Missouri; southern California (varieties occur across this range)

Shade: tolerates partial shade

NOTES
Limits the establishment of invasive species

BES

Appearance
Height: 1.5 to 3 ft.
Flower description: inconspicuous
Flowering period: late May into September

Wildlife Benefits (*Juncus spp.*)
Potential Benefits and Species Served

Food: wildfowl, upland gamebirds, marshbirds, songbirds

Food (bases, roots): muskrat (sparingly), moose

Spawning grounds: rock bass, bluegills, others

Hydrology

Indicator status: Facultative wetland +

Salinity: fresh to brackish water

Tidal zone: upper 25% of the intertidal zone and higher to upland

Nontidal regime: seasonally, regularly, or permanently inundated up to 0.5 ft. or saturated (approximately 13 to 100% of the growing season)

Juncus effusus
Soft rush

Characteristics
Herbaceous / Perennial / Persistent

GROWTH
Rate of spread: slow; less than 0.2 ft. per yr. in unconsolidated sediment
Method of vegetative reproduction: rhizome

PLANTING
Suggested spacing:

For uniform aerial cover	plant at
in 1 yr.	0.5 ft. OC
in 2 yrs.	1.0 ft. OC
in 3 yrs.	1.5 ft. OC

Forms available: seed, rhizome, plug, bare root plant, container

HABITAT
Community: fresh tidal marshes
nontidal marshes
shrub swamps
wet meadows
ditches

Distribution: throughout the United States (varieties occur across this range)

Shade: prefers full sun; may tolerate partial shade

NOTES
Often grows in tussocks or hummocks

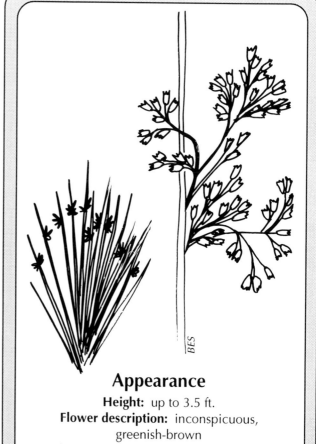

Appearance
Height: up to 3.5 ft.
Flower description: inconspicuous, greenish-brown
Flowering period: July into September

Wildlife Benefits (*Juncus spp.*)
Potential Benefits and Species Served

Food: wildfowl, upland gamebirds, marshbirds, songbirds, waterfowl (including wood duck)

Food (bases, roots): muskrat (sparingly), moose

Spawning grounds: rock bass, bluegills, others

Cover: waterfowl

Hydrology

Indicator status: Facultative wetland +

Salinity: fresh water; less than 0.5 ppt

Tidal zone: upper 10% of intertidal zone to spring tide elevation

Nontidal regime: regularly to permanently inundated up to 1 ft. or saturated (approximately 26 to 100% of the growing season); prefers a period of dry-down

Juncus roemerianus
Black needlerush

Characteristics
Herbaceous / Perennial / Persistent

GROWTH
Rate of spread: moderate; approximately 0.5 ft. per yr. in unconsolidated sediment

Method of vegetative reproduction: rhizome

PLANTING
Suggested spacing:

For uniform ground cover	plant at
in 1 yr.	1 ft. OC
in 2 yrs.	2 ft. OC
in 3 yrs.	3 ft. OC

Forms available: plug, container

HABITAT
Community: brackish and salt marshes

Distribution: southeastern Delaware and Maryland to Florida and Texas

Shade: requires full sun

NOTES
Some nitrogen fixing value

pH preference = 3.5 - 7.2 (tolerates up to 9.5)

Appearance
Height: 1 to 4 ft.

Flower description: inconspicuous, yellow-green

Flowering period: May to October

Wildlife Benefits (*Juncus spp.*)
Potential Benefits and Species Served

Food: wildfowl, upland gamebirds, marshbirds, songbirds

Food (bases, roots): muskrat (sparingly), moose

Spawning grounds: rock bass, bluegills, others

Cover, Nesting: marsh wren

Hydrology
Indicator status: Obligate wetland

Salinity: fresh to salt water; up to 25 ppt

Tidal zone: above mean high water to spring tide elevation

Nontidal regime:

Juncus tenuis
Slender rush

Characteristics
Herbaceous / Perennial

GROWTH
Rate: slow; less than 0.2 ft. per yr. in unconsolidated sediment
Method of vegetative reproduction:

PLANTING
Suggested spacing:

For uniform aerial cover	plant at
in 1 yr.	0.5 ft. OC
in 2 yrs.	1.0 ft. OC
in 3 yrs.	1.5 ft. OC

Forms available: seed

HABITAT
Community: sedge meadows

Distribution: throughout the United States (varieties occur across this range)

Shade: tolerates partial shade

NOTES
Tolerates drought

Appearance
Height: 0.5 to 2 ft.
Flowering period: June to September

Wildlife Benefits (*Juncus spp.*)
Potential Benefits and Species Served

Food: wildfowl, upland gamebirds, marshbirds, songbirds

Food (bases, roots): muskrat (sparingly), moose

Spawning grounds: rock bass, bluegills, others

Hydrology

Indicator status: Facultative –

Salinity: fresh water; less than 0.5 ppt

Tidal zone:

Nontidal regime: irregularly to seasonally inundated or saturated (up to approximately 25% of the growing season)

Juncus torreyi
Torrey rush

Characteristics
Herbaceous / Perennial

GROWTH
Rate of spread: slow; less than 0.2 ft. per yr. in unconsolidated sediment
Method of vegetative reproduction:

PLANTING
Suggested spacing:

For uniform aerial cover	plant at
in 1 yr.	0.5 ft. OC
in 2 yrs.	1.0 ft. OC
in 3 yrs.	1.5 ft. OC

Forms available: seed, bare root plant

HABITAT
Community: sedge meadows

Distribution: Massachusetts to Saskatchewan, south to Alabama and Texas, west to California and northern Mexico

Shade: tolerates partial shade

NOTES
Alkali tolerant
Tolerates drought

BES

Appearance
Height: 1 to 3 ft.
Flowering period: July to October

Wildlife Benefits (*Juncus spp.*)
Potential Benefits and Species Served

Food: wildfowl, upland gamebirds, marshbirds, songbirds

Food (bases, roots): muskrat (sparingly), moose

Spawning grounds: rock bass, bluegills, others

Hydrology

Indicator status: Facultative wetland

Salinity: fresh water; less than 0.5 ppt

Tidal zone:

Nontidal regime: irregularly to seasonally inundated or saturated (up to approximately 25% of the growing season)

Environmental Concern Inc.

Kosteletzkya virginica
Seashore mallow

Characteristics
Herbaceous / Perennial / Nonpersistent

GROWTH
Rate of spread: slow; less than 0.2 ft. per yr. in unconsolidated sediment
Method of vegetative reproduction:

PLANTING
Suggested spacing: irregular intervals throughout an area planted with species which provide full cover
Forms available: container

HABITAT
Community: brackish marshes

Distribution: Long Island south to Florida and Texas (varieties occur across this range)

Shade: requires full sun

NOTES

Appearance
Height: 2 to 4 ft.
Flower color: pink
(large and showy)
Flowering period: July to September

Wildlife Benefits
Potential Benefits and Species Served

Low wildlife value

Hydrology

Indicator status: Obligate wetland

Salinity: brackish water; up to approximately 10 ppt

Tidal zone: above mean high water to spring tide elevation

Nontidal regime:

Leersia oryzoides
Rice cutgrass

Characteristics
Herbaceous / Perennial / Nonpersistent

GROWTH
Rate of spread: moderate; approximately 0.5 ft. per yr. in unconsolidated sediment
Method of vegetative reproduction: rhizome

PLANTING
Suggested spacing:

For uniform ground cover	plant at
in 1 yr.	1 ft. OC
in 2 yrs.	2 ft. OC
in 3 yrs.	3 ft. OC

Forms available: seed, bare root plant, peat pot

HABITAT
Community: fresh tidal marshes
nontidal marshes
wet meadows
ditches and muddy shores

Distribution: Quebec to eastern Washington, south to Florida, Alabama, Louisiana, Texas, New Mexico, Arkansas, and California

Shade: tolerates partial shade

NOTES
Good for sediment stabilization and erosion control
Tolerates drought

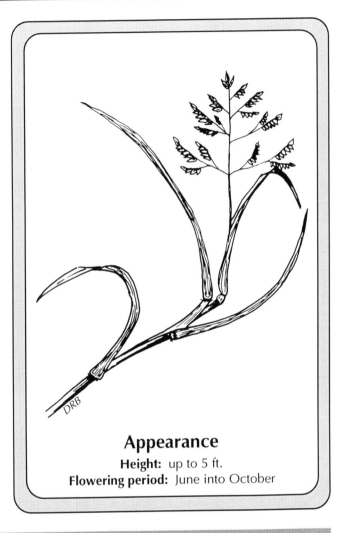

Appearance
Height: up to 5 ft.
Flowering period: June into October

Wildlife Benefits
Potential Benefits and Species Served

Food (seed): many species of duck, swamp and tree sparrow, sora rail

Food source (as a habitat for invertebrates): waterfowl, rails, herons, other birds

Habitat: fish, reptiles, amphibians

Hydrology

Indicator status: Obligate wetland

Salinity: fresh water; less than 0.5 ppt

Tidal zone: upper 10% of intertidal zone and above to spring tide elevation

Nontidal regime: irregularly, seasonally, regularly, or permanently inundated up to 0.5 ft. or saturated (up to 100% of the growing season)

Environmental Concern Inc.

Lobelia cardinalis
Cardinal flower

Characteristics
Herbaceous / Perennial / Nonpersistent

GROWTH
Rate: slow; less than 0.2 ft. per yr. in unconsolidated sediment
Method of vegetative reproduction: shallow rhizome

PLANTING
Suggested spacing: at irregular intervals in clusters throughout an area planted with species which provide full cover
Forms available: seed, bare root plant, container

HABITAT
Community: fresh tidal marshes
nontidal marshes
wooded swamps
seeps
pond, river, and stream banks

Distribution: New Brunswick to Michigan and Minnesota, south to Florida and Texas

Shade: tolerates partial shade

NOTES

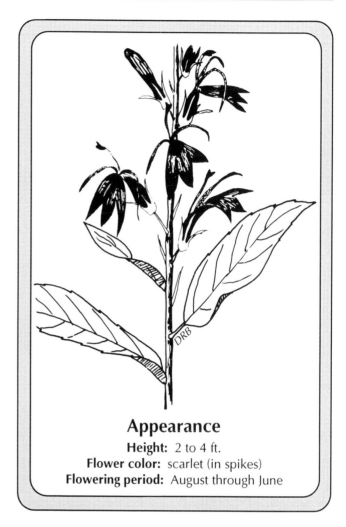

Appearance
Height: 2 to 4 ft.
Flower color: scarlet (in spikes)
Flowering period: August through June

Wildlife Benefits
Potential Benefits and Species Served

Food (Nectar): hummingbird, oriole, butterflies

Hydrology

Indicator status: Facultative wetland +

Salinity: fresh water; less than 0.5 ppt

Tidal zone: upper 10% of the intertidal zone

Nontidal regime: regularly to permanently saturated (approximately 26 to 100% of the growing season)

Lythrum salicaria
Purple loosestrife, Spike lythrum, Salicaire, Bouquet violet

CAUTION: Considered Invasive

Characteristics
Herbaceous / Perennial / Persistent

GROWTH
Rate of spread: rapid; over 1 ft. per yr. in unconsolidated sediment

Method of vegetative reproduction: new shoots from adventitious buds where damaged

PLANTING
Suggested spacing:

For uniform ground cover	plant at
in 1 yr.	2 ft. OC
in 2 yrs.	4 ft. OC
in 3 yrs.	6 ft. OC

Forms available: bare root plant

HABITAT
Community: fresh tidal marshes
nontidal marshes
wet meadows
river and lake borders

Distribution: Quebec and New England to Michigan, south to Virginia

Shade: tolerates partial shade

NOTES
Legislation exists to prevent sale of Purple loosestrife, many land-managers advocate its ban

Re-seeds prolifically

Not native to North America

Appearance
Height: up to 4 ft
Flower color: purple (in spikes)
Flowering period: June through September

Wildlife Benefits
Potential Benefits and Species Served

Low wildlife value

Hydrology

Indicator status: Facultative wetland +

Salinity: fresh water; less than 0.5 pμ

Tidal zone: upper portion of intertidal zone and above to upland elevations

Nontidal regime: irregularly, seasonally, regularly, or permanently inundated up to 0.5 ft or saturated (up to approximately 100% of the growing season)

Nuphar luteum (N. advena)
Spatterdock, Yellow water lily, Cowlily

Characteristics
Herbaceous / Perennial / Nonpersistent

GROWTH
Rate of spread: slow; less than 0.2 ft. per yr. in unconsolidated sediment
Method of vegetative reproduction: rhizome

PLANTING
Suggested spacing:

For uniform aerial cover	plant at
in 1 yr.	0.5 ft. OC
in 2 yrs.	1.0 ft. OC
in 3 yrs.	1.5 ft. OC

Forms available: live bare root, container

HABITAT
Community: fresh tidal marshes
nontidal marshes
swamps
ponds

Distribution: southern Maine to Wisconsin and Nebraska, south to Florida and Texas (varieties occur across this range)

Shade: tolerates partial shade

NOTES
Tolerates acidic water (to pH = 5.0)

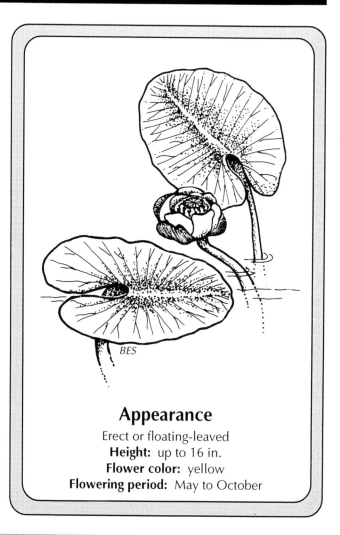

BES

Appearance
Erect or floating-leaved
Height: up to 16 in.
Flower color: yellow
Flowering period: May to October

Wildlife Benefits
Potential Benefits and Species Served

Food (seed): ring-necked, wood, and black ducks

Food (plants): beaver, porcupine, deer, muskrat

Shade, Shelter, Leaves (harbor insects): fish

Hydrology

Indicator status: Obligate wetland

Salinity: resistant; tolerates infrequent flooding by water containing some salt

Tidal zone: below mean low water where average depth is 1 to 3 ft.

Nontidal regime: regularly to permanently inundated from 1 to 3 ft. (approximately 50 to 100% of the growing season); may grow in water which is 6 ft. deep

Onoclea sensibilis
Sensitive fern, Beadfern

Characteristics
Herbaceous / Perennial / Nonpersistent

GROWTH
Rate of spread: moderate; approximately 0.5 ft. per yr. in unconsolidated sediment
Method of vegetative reproduction: rhizome

PLANTING
Suggested spacing:

For uniform ground cover	plant at
in 1 yr.	1 ft. OC
in 2 yrs.	2 ft. OC
in 3 yrs.	3 ft. OC

Forms available: bare root plant, container

HABITAT
Community: fresh tidal marshes
nontidal marshes
wet meadows
forested wetlands (including swamps)
moist woodlands

Distribution: Newfoundland and southern Labrador to Manitoba, south to Florida, Louisiana, and Texas

Shade: tolerates full shade

NOTES
pH preference = 4.5 - 7.5

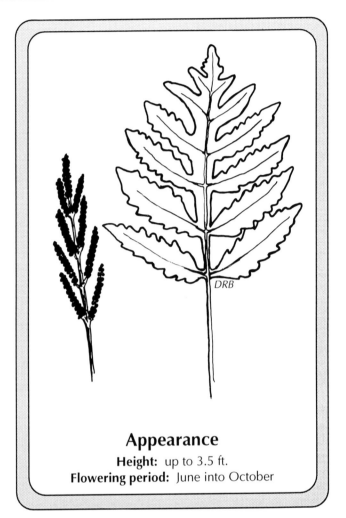

DRB

Appearance
Height: up to 3.5 ft.
Flowering period: June into October

Wildlife Benefits
Potential Benefits and Species Served

Food (leaves): upland gamebirds, mammals (snowshoe hare, deer)

Hydrology

Indicator status: Facultative wetland

Salinity: fresh water; less than 0.5 ppt

Tidal zone:

Nontidal regime: irregularly, seasonally, regularly, or permanently saturated (up to approximately 100% of the growing season)

Osmunda cinnamomea
Cinnamon fern, Buckhorn, Fiddle-heads

Characteristics
Herbaceous / Perennial / Nonpersistent

GROWTH
Rate of spread: slow; less than 0.2 ft. per yr. in unconsolidated sediment
Method of vegetative reproduction: rhizome

PLANTING
Suggested spacing:

For uniform aerial cover	plant at
in 1 yr.	0.5 ft. OC
in 2 yrs.	1.0 ft. OC
in 3 yrs.	1.5 ft. OC

Forms available: bare root plant, container

HABITAT
Community: forested wetlands
   stream banks
   seepage slopes
   bog edges

Distribution: Newfoundland to Minnesota, south to Florida, Texas, and New Mexico

Shade: tolerates full shade, prefers at least partial shade

NOTES
Tolerates drought
Transplants easily

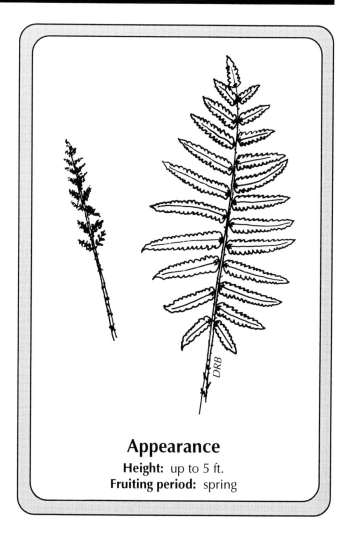

Appearance
Height: up to 5 ft.
Fruiting period: spring

Wildlife Benefits (*Osmunda spp.*)
Potential Benefits and Species Served

Food (leaves): upland gamebirds, mammals (snowshoe hare, deer)

Hydrology

Indicator status: Facultative wetland

Salinity: fresh water; less than 0.5 ppt

Tidal zone:

Nontidal regime: irregularly, seasonally, regularly, or permanently saturated (up to approximately 100% of the growing season)

Osmunda regalis
Royal fern, Flowering fern

Characteristics
Herbaceous / Perennial / Nonpersistent

GROWTH
Rate of spread: slow; less than 0.2 ft. per yr. in unconsolidated sediment
Method of vegetative reproduction: rhizome

PLANTING
Suggested spacing:

For uniform aerial cover	plant at
in 1 yr.	0.5 ft. OC
in 2 yrs.	1.0 ft. OC
in 3 yrs.	1.5 ft. OC

Forms available: bare root plant, container

HABITAT
Community: fresh tidal marshes and swamps
nontidal marshes
swamps
wet meadows
forested wetlands

Distribution: Newfoundland to Saskatchewan, south to Florida, Texas, and Mexico

Shade: tolerates full shade

NOTES
Tolerates drought
Prefers somewhat acidic conditions

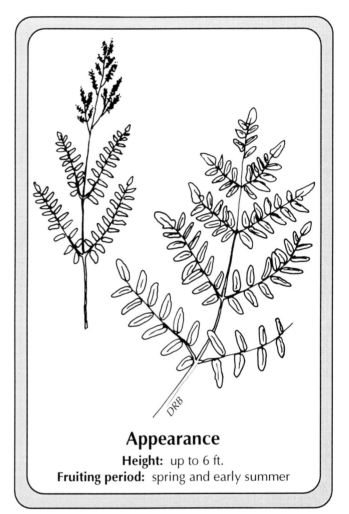

Appearance
Height: up to 6 ft.
Fruiting period: spring and early summer

Wildlife Benefits (*Osmunda spp.*)
Potential Benefits and Species Served

Food (leaves): upland gamebirds, mammals (snowshoe hare, deer)

Hydrology

Indicator status: Obligate wetland

Salinity: fresh water; less than 0.5 ppt

Tidal zone:

Nontidal regime: irregularly, seasonally, regularly, or permanently saturated (up to approximately 100% of the growing season)

Panicum virgatum
Switchgrass

Characteristics
Herbaceous / Perennial / Persistent

GROWTH
Rate of spread: slow; less than 0.2 ft. per yr. in unconsolidated sediment
Method of vegetative reproduction: rhizome

PLANTING
Suggested spacing:

For uniform aerial cover	plant at
in 1 yr.	0.5 ft. OC
in 2 yrs.	1.0 ft. OC
in 3 yrs.	1.5 ft. OC

Forms available: seed, bare root plant, peat or fiber pot

HABITAT
Community: fresh and brackish tidal marshes
nontidal marshes
wet meadows
open woods, prairies, dunes

Distribution: Quebec to Saskatchewan, south to Florida, Texas, and Arizona

Shade: prefers full sun, may tolerate some shade

NOTES
Remains in clumps
Transitional species (buffer)
Tolerates drought

BES

Appearance
Height: up to 6.5 ft.
Flowering period: July to September

Wildlife Benefits
Potential Benefits and Species Served

Food (seeds, young foliage): teals, wigeon, and black duck; snow goose

Food (seeds): snipes, ground dove, bobwhite, wild turkey, red-winged blackbird, cowbird, blue grosbeak, longspurs, sparrows (tree, savannah, Lincoln, etc.), white-footed mouse

Food (plants): muskrat, rabbit, deer

Hydrology

Indicator status: Facultative

Salinity: fresh to brackish water; up to approximately 10 ppt

Tidal zone: above mean high water to upland

Nontidal regime: irregularly to seasonally inundated or saturated (up to approximately 25% of the growing season)

Peltandra virginica
Arrow arum, Tuckahoe, Wampee, Duck corn

Characteristics
Herbaceous / Perennial / Nonpersistent

GROWTH
Rate of spread: slow; less than 0.2 ft. per yr. in unconsolidated sediment
Method of vegetative reproduction: bulb

PLANTING
Suggested spacing:

For uniform aerial cover	plant at
in 1 yr.	0.5 ft. OC
in 2 yrs.	1.0 ft. OC
in 3 yrs.	1.5 ft. OC

Forms available: bare root seedling, dormant bulb, bare root plant, container

HABITAT
Community: fresh to moderately brackish tidal marshes
nontidal marshes
swamps
shallow waters of ponds and lakes

Distribution: southern Maine and southwestern Quebec to Michigan, southern Ontario and Missouri, south to Florida and Texas

Shade: tolerates partial shade

NOTES
pH preference = 5.0 - 6.5
Has shown some allelopathic characteristics

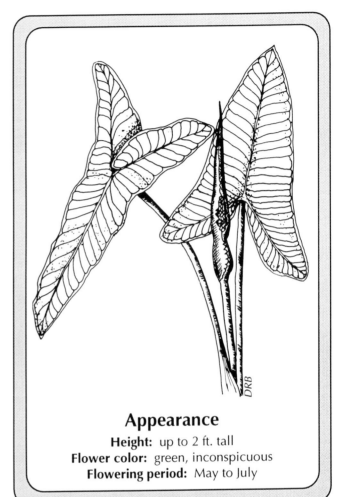

Appearance
Height: up to 2 ft. tall
Flower color: green, inconspicuous
Flowering period: May to July

Wildlife Benefits
Potential Benefits and Species Served

Food (seeds): wood duck (preferred), rail, other marsh and shorebirds

Foliage and rootstocks NOT eaten by geese or muskrat

Hydrology

Indicator status: Obligate wetland

Salinity: fresh to moderately brackish water; up to approximately 1 - 2 ppt

Tidal zone: mid-tide to spring tide elevation

Nontidal regime: regularly to permanently inundated up to 1 ft. or saturated (approximately 25 to 100% of the growing season)

Phalaris arundinacea
Reed canary grass

**CAUTION:
Possibly Invasive**

Characteristics
Herbaceous / Perennial / Persistent

GROWTH
Rate of spread: rapid; over 1 ft. per yr. in unconsolidated sediment
Method of vegetative reproduction: rhizome

PLANTING
Suggested spacing:

For uniform ground cover	plant at
in 1 yr.	2 ft. OC
in 2 yrs.	4 ft. OC
in 3 yrs.	6 ft. OC

Forms available: seed, bare root plant

HABITAT
Community: fresh tidal marshes
nontidal marshes
stream banks
lake shores
moist woods

Distribution: Newfoundland to southern Alaska, south to North Carolina, Kansas, and southern California

Shade: requires full sun

NOTES
Tolerates drought
Soil stabilizer
Should not be used in soil stabilization for temporarily exposed pond bottoms or where open water habitat is desired. Upon flooding, may form floating aquatic mats. (Lefor 1987)

Appearance
Height: up to 5 ft.
Flowering period: June through August

Wildlife Benefits
Potential Benefits and Species Served

Food, Cover: prairie vole, birds

Nesting: marsh wren, red-winged blackbird

Brood cover: wood duck

Hydrology

Indicator status: Facultative wetland +

Salinity: fresh water; less than 0.5 ppt

Tidal zone:

Nontidal regime: seasonally to regulary inundated up to 1 ft., permanently inundated up to 0.5 ft., or saturated (approximately 13 to 100% of the growing season)

Phragmites australis
Common reed, Wild reed

**CAUTION:
Considered Invasive**

Characteristics
Herbaceous / Perennial / Persistent

GROWTH
Rate of spread: rapid; over 1 ft. per yr. in unconsolidated sediment (can spread up to 30 ft. in one yr.)
Method of vegetative reproduction: rhizome

PLANTING
Suggested spacing:

For uniform ground cover	plant at
in 1 yr.	2 ft. OC
in 2 yrs.	4 ft. OC
in 3 yrs.	6 ft. OC

Forms available: bare root plant

HABITAT
Community: fresh and brackish tidal marshes
nontidal marshes
swamps
wet shores
ditches and disturbed areas

Distribution: Nova Scotia and Quebec to British Columbia, south to Florida, Texas, and California

Shade: requires full sun

NOTES
Highly invasive; considered a pest species in many states
Good sediment stabilizer for extreme cases of erosion
pH preference = 3.7 – 9.0
Has shown some allelopathic characteristics

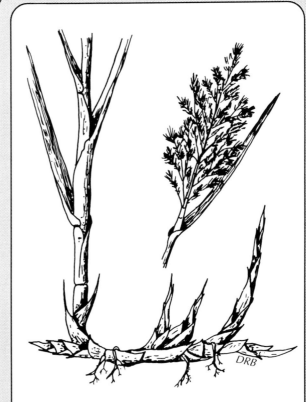

Appearance
Height: up to 10 ft.
Flowering period: June into September

Wildlife Benefits
Potential Benefits and Species Served

Cover: upland gamebirds, songbirds, marshbirds, shorebirds, aquatic furbearers, terrestrial furbearers

Low food value

Hydrology

Indicator status: Facultative wetland

Salinity: fresh to brackish water; up to 20 ppt

Tidal zone: in salt marsh, above mean high water to spring tide elevation; in fresh marsh, upper 50% of intertidal zone

Nontidal regime: seasonally, regularly, or permanently inundated up to 2 ft. or saturated (approximately 13 to 100% of the growing season)

Polygonum hydropiperoides
Marsh smartweed, Mild water pepper

Characteristics
Herbaceous / Perennial / Nonpersistent

GROWTH
Rate of spread:
Method of vegetative reproduction: creeping rootstocks

PLANTING
Suggested spacing:
Forms available: seed, plug

HABITAT
Community: fresh tidal marshes
wet meadows

Distribution: Nova Scotia to British Columbia, south throughout the United States (varieties occur across this range)

Shade: tolerates partial shade

NOTES

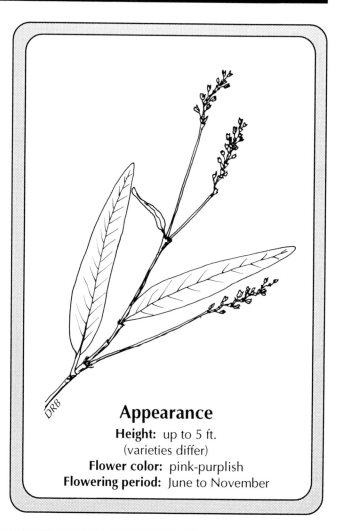

Appearance
Height: up to 5 ft.
(varieties differ)
Flower color: pink-purplish
Flowering period: June to November

Wildlife Benefits
Potential Benefits and Species Served

Food: northern pintail, wild turkey

Brood cover: wood duck

Food source (as habitat for invertebrates): waterfowl, rails, herons, other birds

Hydrology

Indicator status: Obligate wetland

Salinity: fresh water; less than 0.5 ppt

Tidal zone:

Nontidal regime: regularly to permanently inundated up to 1 ft. or saturated (approximately 26 to 100% of the growing season)

Polygonum pensylvanicum
Pennsylvania smartweed, Pinkweed, Giant smartweed

Characteristics
Herbaceous / Annual / Nonpersistent

GROWTH
Rate of spread:
Method of vegetative reproduction: none

PLANTING
Suggested spacing:
Forms available: seed, container

HABITAT
Community: freshwater marshes
wet meadows

Distribution: Nova Scotia and Quebec to Minnesota
and South Dakota, south to Florida and Texas
(varieties occur across this range)

Shade: requires full sun

NOTES
Tolerates poor soil fertility
Good for erosion control

Appearance
Height: up to 6.5 ft.
Flower color: pink or purplish
Flowering period: May through October

Wildlife Benefits
Potential Benefits and Species Served

Food, Cover: wood duck, northern pintail, black duck,
wild turkey

Food (seeds): waterfowl, marshbirds, shorebirds,
songbirds, upland game birds, aquatic and terrestrial
furbearers, small mammals

Hydrology

Indicator status: Facultative wetland

Salinity: fresh water; less than 0.5 ppt

Tidal zone: mean high water and above to upland

Nontidal regime: regularly to permanently inundated up to 0.5 ft. or saturated (approximately 26 to 100% of the growing season)

Polygonum persicaria
Lady's thumb, Heart's ease

Characteristics
Herbaceous / Annual / Nonpersistent

GROWTH
Rate of spread:
Method of vegetative reproduction: none

PLANTING
Suggested spacing:
Forms available:

HABITAT
Community: freshwater marshes
wet meadows
moist soils

Distribution: throughout the United States (varieties occur across this range)

Shade:

NOTES

Appearance
Height: up to 3 ft.
Flower color: pink-purplish or green
Flowering period: June to October

Wildlife Benefits
Potential Benefits and Species Served

High food value

Cover, Food (seeds): songbirds, gamebirds (wild turkey)

Rhizomes: rice rat, Canada goose

Hydrology

Indicator status: Facultative wetland

Salinity: fresh water; less than 0.5 ppt

Tidal zone:

Nontidal regime: seasonally to regularly inundated up to 1 ft. or saturated (approximately 13 to 75% of the growing season)

Polygonum punctatum
Marsh smartweed, Red top, Dotted smartweed

Characteristics
Herbaceous / Perennial / Nonpersistant

GROWTH
Rate of spread:
Method of vegetative reproduction:

PLANTING
Suggested spacing:
Forms available: bare root plant

HABITAT
Community: fresh tidal marshes
nontidal marshes

Distribution: Quebec to British Columbia, south to
Florida and California (varieties occur across this
range)

Shade:

NOTES
Tolerates mildly alkaline soils

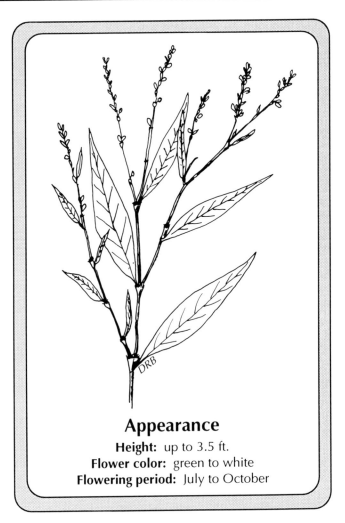

Appearance
Height: up to 3.5 ft.
Flower color: green to white
Flowering period: July to October

Wildlife Benefits
Potential Benefits and Species Served

Food (seeds): waterfowl, marshbirds, shorebirds, upland
gamebirds, songbirds, aquatic furbearers, small
mammals

Hydrology

Indicator status: Obligate wetland

Salinity: fresh water; less than 0.5 ppt

Tidal zone: upper 50% of intertidal zone

Nontidal regime: regularly to permanently inundated or saturated (approximately 26 to 100% of
the growing season)

Pontederia cordata
Pickerelweed

Characteristics
Herbaceous / Perennial / Nonpersistant

GROWTH
Rate of spread: moderate; approximately 0.5 ft. per yr. in unconsolidated sediment
Method of vegetative reproduction: rhizome

PLANTING
Suggested spacing:

For uniform ground cover	plant at
in 1 yr.	1 ft. OC
in 2 yrs.	2 ft. OC
in 3 yrs.	3 ft. OC

Forms available: dormant rhizome, bare root plant, container, peat or fiber pot

HABITAT
Community: fresh to moderately brackish tidal marshes
nontidal marshes
shallow water of ponds and lakes

Distribution: Nova Scotia to Ontario and Minnesota, south to northern Florida and Texas

Shade: tolerates partial shade

NOTES
pH preference = 6.0 - 8.0
Loses much water through transpiration

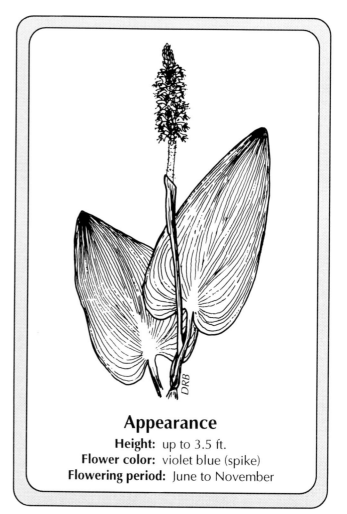

Appearance
Height: up to 3.5 ft.
Flower color: violet blue (spike)
Flowering period: June to November

Wildlife Benefits
Potential Benefits and Species Served

Food (seed): mottled duck, other waterfowl

Food (foliage, rootstock): Canada goose, muskrat

Cover: fish

Hydrology

Indicator status: Obligate wetland

Salinity: fresh to moderately brackish water; up to approximately 3 ppt

Tidal zone: upper 50% of the intertidal zone

Nontidal regime: regularly to permanently inundated up to 1 ft. or saturated (approximately 26 to 100% of the growing season)

Rumex verticillatus
Water dock, Swamp dock

Characteristics
Herbaceous / Perennial / Nonpersistent

GROWTH
Rate of spread: slow; less than 0.2 ft. per yr. in unconsolidated sediment
Method of vegetative reproduction: rhizome

PLANTING
Suggested spacing: at irregular intervals throughout an area planted with species which provide full cover
Forms available: seed

HABITAT
Community: fresh tidal marshes
nontidal marshes
swamps
stream edges

Distribution: Quebec and Ontario to Wisconsin and Kansas, south to Florida and Texas

Shade:

NOTES
Readily propagated from rhizomes

BES

Appearance
Height: up to 3.5 ft.
Flower color: green, tinged with red
Flowering period: June to September

Wildlife Benefits
Potential Benefits and Species Served

Food (seeds): cinnamon teal, ruffed grouse, red-winged blackbird, hoary redpoll; grasshopper, song, swamp, tree, and white-crowned sparrows

Food (leaves, plants): deer, cottontail rabbit

Hydrology

Indicator status: Obligate wetland

Salinity: fresh water; less than 0.5 ppt

Tidal zone: upper 50% of intertidal zone

Nontidal regime: regularly to permanently inundated up to 0.5 ft. or saturated (approximately 26 to 100% of the growing season)

Sagittaria graminae
Grass-like duck potato

Characteristics
Herbaceous / Perennial / Nonpersistent

GROWTH
Rate of spread:
Method of vegetative reproduction: stolon

PLANTING
Suggested spacing:
Forms available: bare root plant

HABITAT
Community: fresh or brackish tidal marshes
nontidal marshes
pond edges

Distribution: Newfoundland and Labrador to Ontario
south to Florida and Texas, west to Ohio, Indiana,
Missouri, and Illinois (varieties occur across this
range)

Shade:

NOTES
Forms clumps
pH preference is approximately 7.0
Loses much water through transpiration
Has shown some allelopathic characteristics; may be
allelopathic towards *Hydrilla verticillata*

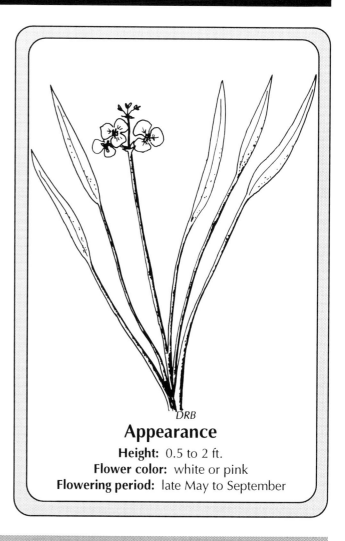

DRB

Appearance
Height: 0.5 to 2 ft.
Flower color: white or pink
Flowering period: late May to September

Wildlife Benefits
Potential Benefits and Species Served

Food: crayfish, mallard, pintail, mottled duck, other
waterfowl, nutria, swamp rabbit, beaver

Hydrology
Indicator status: Obligate wetland
Salinity: fresh to brackish water

Tidal zone:

Nontidal regime: regularly to permanently inundated up to 1 ft. or saturated (approximately 26 to 100% of the growing season)

Sagittaria latifolia
Duck potato, Big-leaved arrowhead, Wapato

Characteristics
Herbaceous / Perennial / Nonpersistent

GROWTH
Rate of spread: rapid; over 1 ft. per yr. in unconsolidated sediment
Method of vegetative reproduction: runners, tubers

PLANTING
Suggested spacing:

For uniform ground cover	plant at
in 1 yr.	2 ft. OC
in 2 yrs.	4 ft. OC
in 3 yrs.	6 ft. OC

Forms available: tuber, bare root plant, container

HABITAT
Community: fresh tidal marshes
nontidal marshes
swamps
forested seeps
borders of streams, lakes, ponds

Distribution: New Brunswick to southern British Columbia, south to Florida, California, and Mexico (varieties occur across this range)

Shade: tolerates partial shade

NOTES
Loses much water through transpiration

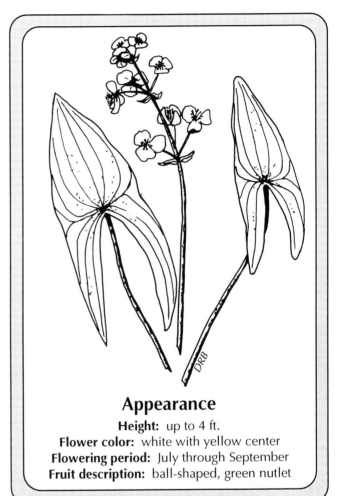

Appearance
Height: up to 4 ft.
Flower color: white with yellow center
Flowering period: July through September
Fruit description: ball-shaped, green nutlet

Wildlife Benefits
Potential Benefits and Species Served

Food (seeds, tubers, plants): ducks: canvasback, gadwall, scaup, black, mallard, pintail, and ring-necked; trumpeter and whistling swans, rails, muskrat, beaver

Caution: mallard ducks and muskrat can very rapidly consume tubers planted in an area.

Hydrology

Indicator status: Obligate wetland

Salinity: fresh water; less than 0.5 ppt

Tidal zone: upper 50% of the intertidal zone

Nontidal regime: regularly to permanently inundated up to 2 ft. or saturated (approximately 26 to 100% of the growing season)

Sagittaria rigida
Deep water duck potato

Characteristics
Herbaceous / Perennial / Nonpersistent

GROWTH
Rate of spread:
Method of vegetative reproduction: runners, tubers

PLANTING
Suggested spacing:
Forms available: tuber, bare root plant

HABITAT
Community: fresh and brackish tidal marshes;
nontidal marshes;
swamps;
ponds

Distribution: southwestern Quebec, southern Maine to Minnesota, south to Virginia, Kentucky, Tennessee, Missouri, Nebraska

Shade:

NOTES
Forms clumps

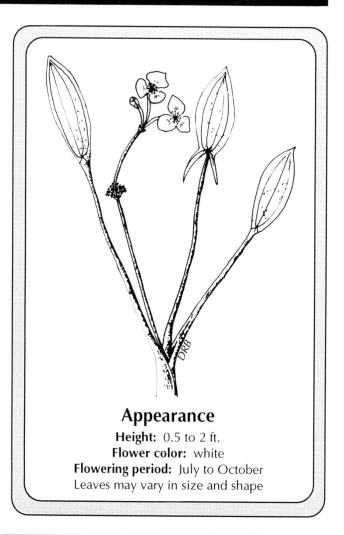

Appearance
Height: 0.5 to 2 ft.
Flower color: white
Flowering period: July to October
Leaves may vary in size and shape

Wildlife Benefits
Potential Benefits and Species Served

Food (seeds, tubers, plants): waterfowl, aquatic furbearers (e.g., beaver, muskrat)

Food (seeds): marshbirds, shorebirds

Cover: minnows, young amphibians

Hydrology

Indicator status: Obligate wetland

Salinity: fresh to slightly brackish water; up to approximately 2 ppt

Tidal zone: upper 50% of intertidal zone

Nontidal regime: regularly to permanently inundated from 1 to 3 ft. (approximately 26 to 100% of the growing season); tolerates fluctuating water levels

Salicornia virginica
Pickleweed, Pacific glasswort, Perennial pickleweed, Perennial glasswort, Woody glasswort

Characteristics
Hebaceous / Perennial / Nonpersistent

GROWTH
Rate of spread: rapid; over 1 ft. per yr. in unconsolidated sediment
Method of vegetative reproduction: rhizome

PLANTING
Suggested spacing: in the northeastern part of the country this plant grows intermittently among other high marsh vegetation; it is not recommended that it be planted in a monostand, but rather to add diversity
Forms available:

HABITAT
Community: salt and brackish tidal marshes
Distribution: southern New Hampshire to Florida and Texas; also Alaska to California
Shade: requires full sun

NOTES
Establishes quickly
pH preference is approximately 8.0
Often found in poorly drained depressions in salt marshes

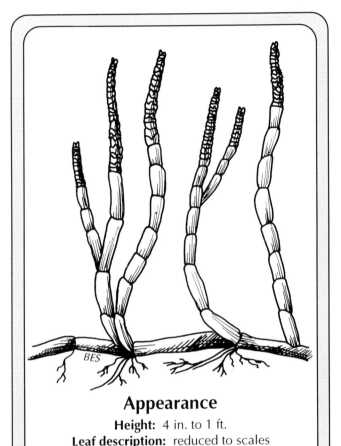

Appearance
Height: 4 in. to 1 ft.
Leaf description: reduced to scales
Flower description: green, inconspicuous
Flowering period: August into October

Wildlife Benefits
Potential Benefits and Species Served

Cover: salt marsh harvest mouse, shrew

Hydrology

Indicator status: Obligate wetland

Salinity: brackish to salt water; up to 60 ppt

Tidal zone: above mean high water to spring tide elevation

Nontidal regime:

Saururus cernuus
Lizard tail

Characteristics
Herbaceous / Perennial / Nonpersistent

GROWTH
Rate of spread: rapid; over 1 ft. per yr. in unconsolidated sediment
Method of vegetative reproduction: rhizome

PLANTING
Suggested spacing:

For uniform ground cover	plant at
in 1 yr.	2 ft. OC
in 2 yrs.	4 ft. OC
in 3 yrs.	6 ft. OC

Forms available: rhizome, bare root plant, container

HABITAT
Community: fresh tidal marshes and swamps
nontidal marshes and swamps
shallow waters

Distribution: southern New England, southern Quebec and Minnesota, south to Florida and Texas

Shade: tolerates partial shade

NOTES

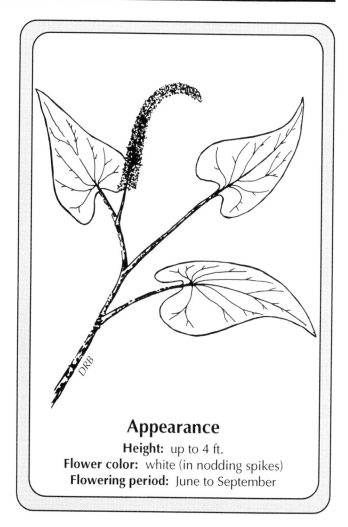

Appearance
Height: up to 4 ft.
Flower color: white (in nodding spikes)
Flowering period: June to September

Wildlife Benefits
Potential Benefits and Species Served

Food: wood duck

Hydrology

Indicator status: Obligate wetland

Salinity: fresh water; less than 0.5 ppt

Tidal zone:

Nontidal regime: regularly to permanently inundated up to 1 ft. or saturated (approximately 26 to 100% of the growing season)

Scirpus acutus
Hardstem bulrush, Common tule

Characteristics
Herbaceous / Perennial / Nonpersistent

GROWTH
Rate of spread:
Method of vegetative reproduction: rhizome

PLANTING
Suggested spacing:
Forms available: seed, rhizome

HABITAT
Community: brackish and fresh tidal marshes
nontidal marshes
shores

Distribution: Newfoundland to British Columbia south to Nova Scotia, New England, northern New Jersey, Pennsylvania, Ohio, Indiana, Illinois, Missouri, Oklahoma, Texas, New Mexico, Arizona, and California

Shade:

NOTES
Good for sediment stabilization and erosion control

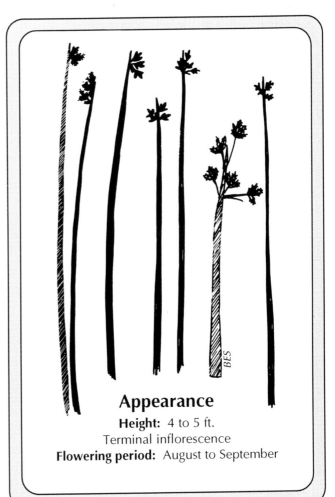

Appearance
Height: 4 to 5 ft.
Terminal inflorescence
Flowering period: August to September

Wildlife Benefits (*Scirpus spp.*)
Potential Benefits and Species Served

Cover and Food (seeds or rhizomes): ducks: wigeon, black, canvasback, gadwall, mallard, mottled, pintail, redhead, ring-necked, ruddy, greater and lesser scaups, shoveler, and blue-winged, cinnamon, and green-winged teals; Canada and snow geese, trumpeter swan, sandhill crane, long-billed dowitcher, Hudsonian godwit, sora and Virginia rails, semipalmated sandpiper, snipe, muskrat, fish

Nesting: bluegills, largemouth bass

Hydrology

Indicator status: Obligate wetland

Salinity: fresh to brackish water

Tidal zone: upper 50% of the intertidal zone and above to spring tide elevation

Nontidal regime: regularly to permanently inundated up to 3 ft. or saturated (approximately 25 to 100% of the growing season)

Scirpus americanus (S. olneyi)
Olney's bulrush, Olney three-square

Characteristics
Herbaceous / Perennial / Semi-persistent

GROWTH
Rate of spread: rapid; over 1 ft. per yr. in unconsolidated sediment
Method of vegetative reproduction: rhizome

PLANTING
Suggested spacing:

For uniform ground cover	plant at
in 1 yr.	2 ft. OC
in 2 yrs.	4 ft. OC
in 3 yrs.	6 ft. OC

Forms available: rhizome, bare root plant, container

HABITAT
Community: brackish tidal marshes
nontidal alkali marshes

Distribution: New Hampshire and western Nova Scotia to Florida and Mexico, inland New York, Minnesota, and western states

Shade: prefers full sun

NOTES
Tolerates drought/dry-down

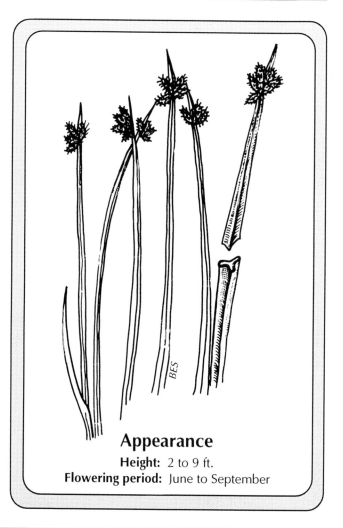

Appearance
Height: 2 to 9 ft.
Flowering period: June to September

Wildlife Benefits (*Scirpus spp.*)
Potential Benefits and Species Served

Cover and Food (seeds or rhizomes): ducks: wigeon, black, canvasback, gadwall, mallard, mottled, pintail, redhead, ring-necked, ruddy, greater and lesser scaups, shoveler, and blue-winged, cinnamon, and green-winged teals; Canada and snow geese, trumpeter swan, sandhill crane, long-billed dowitcher, Hudsonian godwit, sora and Virginia rails, semipalmated sandpiper, snipe, muskrat, fish

Nesting: bluegills, largemouth bass

Hydrology

Indicator status: Obligate wetland

Salinity: brackish water; up to approximately 15 ppt

Tidal zone: upper 50% of the intertidal zone and above to spring tide elevation

Nontidal regime: regularly to permanently inundated up to 0.5 ft. or saturated (approximately 26 to 100% of the growing season)

Scirpus cyperinus
Wool grass

Characteristics
Herbaceous / Perennial / Persistent

GROWTH
Rate of spread: moderate; approximately 0.5 ft. per yr. in unconsolidated sediment
Method of vegetative reproduction: rhizome

PLANTING
Suggested spacing:

For uniform ground cover	plant at
in 1 yr.	1 ft. OC
in 2 yrs.	2 ft. OC
in 3 yrs.	3 ft. OC

Forms available: seed, rhizome, bare root plant, container

HABITAT
Community: fresh tidal marshes
nontidal marshes
swamps and Forested seasonal wetlands
wet meadows
swales and ditches
sloughs, ponds, bogs

Distribution: Newfoundland to Minnesota, south to Florida and Louisiana

Shade: requires full sun

NOTES
Tolerates drought
pH preference = 5.0 - 8.0 (may tolerate as low as 3.7)
Colonizes disturbed areas

Appearance
Height: 4 to 6.5 ft.
Brown drooping inflorescence
Flowering period: August through September

Wildlife Benefits (*Scirpus spp.*)
Potential Benefits and Species Served

Cover and Food (seeds or rhizomes): ducks: wigeon, black, canvasback, gadwall, mallard, mottled, pintail, redhead, ring-necked, ruddy, greater and lesser scaups, shoveler, and blue-winged, cinnamon, and green-winged teals; Canada and snow geese, trumpeter swan, sandhill crane, long-billed dowitcher, Hudsonian godwit, sora and Virginia rails, semipalmated sandpiper, snipe, muskrat, fish

Nesting: bluegills, largemouth bass

Hydrology

Indicator status: Facultative wetland +

Salinity: fresh water; less than 0.5 ppt

Tidal zone:

Nontidal regime: irregularly to seasonally inundated or saturated (up to 25% of the growing season)

Scirpus fluviatilis
River bulrush

Characteristics
Herbaceous / Perennial / Nonpersistent

GROWTH
Rate of spread: moderate; approximately 0.5 ft. per yr. in unconsolidated sediment
Method of vegetative reproduction: rhizome

PLANTING
Suggested spacing:

For uniform ground cover	plant at
in 1 yr.	1 ft. OC
in 2 yrs.	2 ft. OC
in 3 yrs.	3 ft. OC

Forms available: bare root plant

HABITAT
Community: nontidal marshes
lake and pond edges

Distribution: western New Brunswick to Saskatchewan and Washington, south to northeastern Virginia, Ohio, Indiana, Illinois, Missouri, Kansas, New Mexico, California

Shade: tolerates partial shade

NOTES
Good for erosion control

Appearance
Height: 2 to 6 ft.
Flowering period: July to September

Wildlife Benefits (*Scirpus spp.*)
Potential Benefits and Species Served

Cover and Food (seeds or rhizomes): ducks: wigeon, black, canvasback, gadwall, mallard, mottled, pintail, redhead, ring-necked, ruddy, greater and lesser scaups, shoveler, and blue-winged, cinnamon, and green-winged teals; Canada and snow geese, trumpeter swan, sandhill crane, long-billed dowitcher, Hudsonian godwit, sora and Virginia rails, semipalmated sandpiper, snipe, muskrat, fish

Nesting: bluegills, largemouth bass

Hydrology

Indicator status: Obligate wetland

Salinity: fresh water; less than 0.5 ppt

Tidal zone:

Nontidal regime: regularly to permanently inundated up to 1.0 ft. or saturated (approximately 26 to 100% of the growing season but prefers areas with some period of dry-down)

Scirpus pungens (S. americanus)
Common three square, Chair-maker's rush, Sword grass

Characteristics
Herbaceous / Perennial / Semi-persistent

GROWTH
Rate of spread: rapid; over 1 ft. per yr. in unconsolidated sediment
Method of vegetative reproduction: rhizome

PLANTING
Suggested spacing:

For uniform ground cover	plant at
in 1 yr.	2 ft. OC
in 2 yrs.	4 ft. OC
in 3 yrs.	6 ft. OC

Forms available: dormant rhizome, bare root plant, peat pot, container

HABITAT
Community: brackish and fresh tidal marshes
nontidal marshes
wet sandy shores
coastal dunes

Distribution: Newfoundland, Quebec, Minnesota, and Nebraska, south to Florida and Texas

Shade: requires full sun

NOTES
Soil stabilizer
Tolerates drought
Prefers neutral soil

Appearance
Height: up to 4 ft.
Flowering period: June to September

Wildlife Benefits (*Scirpus spp.*)
Potential Benefits and Species Served

Cover and Food (seeds or rhizomes): ducks: wigeon, black, canvasback, gadwall, mallard, mottled, pintail, redhead, ring-necked, ruddy, greater and lesser scaups, shoveler, and blue-winged, cinnamon, and green-winged teals; Canada and snow geese, trumpeter swan, sandhill crane, long-billed dowitcher, Hudsonian godwit, sora and Virginia rails, semipalmated sandpiper, snipe, muskrat, fish

Nesting: bluegills, largemouth bass

Hydrology
Indicator status: Facultative wetland +

Salinity: fresh to brackish water; up to 15 ppt

Tidal zone: upper 50% of intertidal zone to spring tide elevation

Nontidal regime: seasonally, regularly, or permanently inundated up to 0.5 ft. or saturated (approximately 13 to 100% of the growing season)

Scirpus robustus
Saltmeadow bulrush, Alkali bulrush

Characteristics
Herbaceous / Perennial / Nonpersistent

GROWTH
Rate of spread: moderate; approximately 0.5 ft. per yr. in unconsolidated sediment
Method of vegetative reproduction: rhizome

PLANTING
Suggested spacing:

For uniform ground cover	plant at
in 1 yr.	1 ft. OC
in 2 yrs.	2 ft. OC
in 3 yrs.	3 ft. OC

Forms available: bare root plant, peat pot

HABITAT
Community: brackish or salt marshes

Distribution: Nova Scotia to Florida and Texas; California

Shade: requires full sun

NOTES
pH preference = 4.0 - 6.9

Appearance
Height: up to 5 ft.
Flowering period: July to October

Wildlife Benefits (*Scirpus spp.*)
Potential Benefits and Species Served

Cover and Food (seeds or rhizomes): ducks: wigeon, black, canvasback, gadwall, mallard, mottled, pintail, redhead, ring-necked, ruddy, greater and lesser scaups, shoveler, and blue-winged, cinnamon, and green-winged teals; Canada and snow geese, trumpeter swan, sandhill crane, long-billed dowitcher, Hudsonian godwit, sora and Virginia rails, semipalmated sandpiper, snipe, muskrat, fish

Nesting: bluegills, largemouth bass

Hydrology
Indicator status: Obligate wetland

Salinity: brackish to salt water; up to 25 ppt (does best in fluctuating salinity)

Tidal zone: upper 10% of intertidal zone and above to spring tide elevation

Nontidal regime:

Scirpus validus
Soft stem bulrush

Characteristics
Herbaceous / Perennial / Nonpersistent

GROWTH
Rate of spread: rapid; over 1 ft. per yr. in unconsolidated sediment

Method of vegetative reproduction: rhizome

PLANTING
Suggested spacing:

For uniform ground cover	plant at
in 1 yr.	2 ft. OC
in 2 yrs.	4 ft. OC
in 3 yrs.	6 ft. OC

Forms available: seed, dormant rhizome, bare root plant, container

HABITAT
Community: brackish and fresh tidal marshes
nontidal marshes
shores

Distribution: Newfoundland to southern Alaska, south to Florida, Oklahoma, Texas, New Mexico, northern Mexico, California

Shade: requires full sun

NOTES
pH preference = 6.5 - 8.5

Appearance
Height: up to 10 ft.
Flowering period: June to September

Wildlife Benefits (*Scirpus spp.*)
Potential Benefits and Species Served

Cover and Food (seeds or rhizomes): ducks: wigeon, black, canvasback, gadwall, mallard, mottled, pintail, redhead, ring-necked, ruddy, greater and lesser scaups, shoveler, and blue-winged, cinnamon, and green-winged teals; Canada and snow geese, trumpeter swan, sandhill crane, long-billed dowitcher, Hudsonian godwit, sora and Virginia rails, semipalmated sandpiper, snipe, muskrat, fish

Nesting: bluegills, largemouth bass

Hydrology

Indicator status: Obligate wetland

Salinity: fresh to brackish water; up to approximately 5 ppt

Tidal zone: upper 50% of intertidal zone to spring tide elevation

Nontidal regime: regularly to permanently inundated up to 1 ft. or saturated (approximately 26 to 100% of the growing season)

Sium suave

Water parsnip

Characteristics

Herbaceous / Perennial / Nonpersistent

GROWTH

Rate of spread: slow; less than 0.2 ft. per yr. in unconsolidated sediment

Method of vegetative reproduction:

PLANTING

Suggested spacing: it is not suggested that this species be used to create uniform cover, but rather to add diversity; space at irregular intervals throughout an area planted with species which provide full cover

Forms available:

HABITAT

Community: fresh tidal marshes
slightly brackish marshes
nontidal marshes
swamps
muddy shores

Distribution: Newfoundland to British Columbia, south to Florida, Louisiana, and California

Shade:

NOTES

Tolerates dry-down

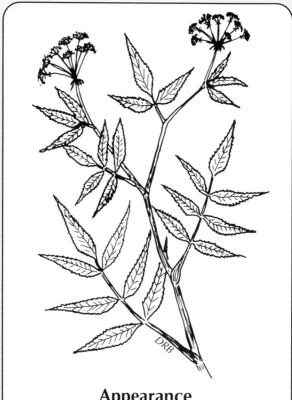

Appearance

Height: up to 7 ft.
Flower color: white (in compound umbels)
Flowering period: July through September

Wildlife Benefits

Potential Benefits and Species Served

(information not available)

Hydrology

Indicator status: Obligate wetland

Salinity: fresh to slightly brackish water

Tidal zone:

Nontidal regime: regularly to permanently inundated up to 0.5 ft. or saturated (approximately 26 to 100% of the growing season)

Sparganium americanum
Eastern or Lesser bur-reed

Characteristics
Herbaceous / Perennial / Nonpersistent

GROWTH
Rate of spread: rapid; over 1 ft. per yr. in unconsolidated sediment

Method of vegetative reproduction: rhizome

PLANTING
Suggested spacing:

For uniform ground cover	plant at
in 1 yr.	2 ft. OC
in 2 yrs.	4 ft. OC
in 3 yrs.	6 ft. OC

Forms available: bare root plant

HABITAT
Community: nontidal marshes
shallow waters
muddy shores

Distribution: Newfoundland and Quebec to Minnesota, south to Florida and Louisiana

Shade: tolerates partial shade

NOTES
Stabilizes wave-beaten shorelines and flats

Appearance
Height: up to 5 ft.
Flower description: greenish in ball-shaped heads
Flowering period: May through August

Wildlife Benefits
Potential Benefits and Species Served

Food (seeds): ducks: mallard, wood, canvasback, ring-necked, scaups, and teals; whistling swan, muskrat, beaver

Food (plants): muskrat, Canada goose

Hydrology

Indicator status: Obligate wetland

Salinity: fresh water; less than 0.5 ppt

Tidal zone:

Nontidal regime: regularly to permanently inundated up to 0.5 ft. or saturated (approximately 26 to 100% of the growing season)

Sparganium eurycarpum
Great or Giant bur-reed

Characteristics
Herbaceous / Perennial / Nonpersistent

GROWTH
Rate of spread: rapid; over 1 ft. per yr. in unconsolidated sediment
Method of vegetative reproduction: rhizome

PLANTING
Suggested spacing:

For uniform ground cover	plant at
in 1 yr.	2 ft. OC
in 2 yrs.	4 ft. OC
in 3 yrs.	6 ft. OC

Forms available: seed, rhizome, bare root plant, peat pot, container

HABITAT
Community: nontidal marshes
shallow waters
swamps
muddy shores

Distribution: Quebec and Nova Scotia to southern British Columbia, south to Florida, Ohio, Indiana, Illinois, Missouri, Kansas, Colorado, Utah, California

Shade: tolerates partial shade

NOTES
Good for shoreline stabilization

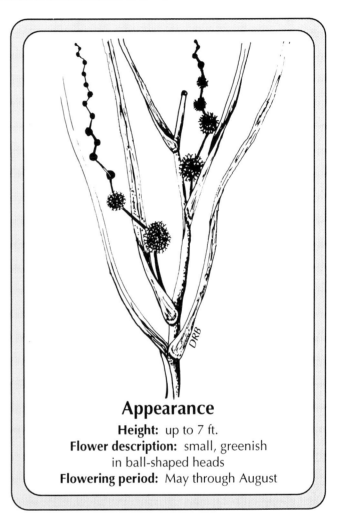

Appearance
Height: up to 7 ft.
Flower description: small, greenish in ball-shaped heads
Flowering period: May through August

Wildlife Benefits
Potential Benefits and Species Served

Food (seeds): black duck, wood duck, other waterfowl, whistling swan, pheasant, beaver

Food (plants): muskrat, Canada goose, deer

Cover: marshbirds, waterfowl

Hydrology

Indicator status: Obligate wetland

Salinity: fresh water; less than 0.5 ppt

Tidal zone:

Nontidal regime: regularly to permanently inundated up to 1 ft. or saturated (approximately 26 to 100% of the growing season)

Spartina alterniflora
Smooth cordgrass, Salt marsh cordgrass

Characteristics
Herbaceous / Perennial / Semipersistent

GROWTH
Rate of spread: rapid; over 1 ft. per yr. in unconsolidated sediment
Method of vegetative reproduction: rhizome

PLANTING
Suggested spacing:

For uniform ground cover	plant at
in 1 yr.	2 ft. OC
in 2 yrs.	4 ft. OC
in 3 yrs.	6 ft. OC

Forms available: seed, bare root plant, peat pot

HABITAT
Community: tidal salt and brackish marshes

Distribution: Quebec and Newfoundland to Florida and Texas (varieties occur across this range)

Shade: requires full sun

NOTES
Excellent for sediment stabilization

Plants native to Maine and Massachusetts are known to be genetically isolated from plants native to the range from Connecticut to the Carolinas

pH range = 4.5 - 8.5

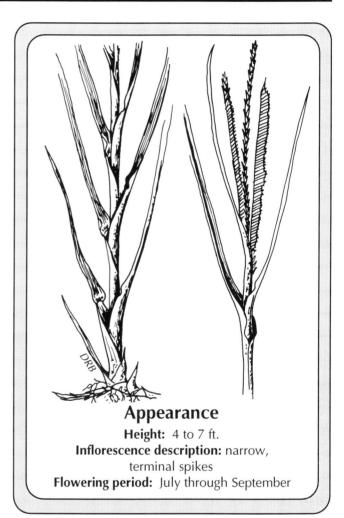

Appearance
Height: 4 to 7 ft.
Inflorescence description: narrow, terminal spikes
Flowering period: July through September

Wildlife Benefits
Potential Benefits and Species Served

Food (seeds, plant parts, rootstocks): black duck, Canada and snow geese, rails, seaside and sharp-tailed sparrows, muskrat

Hydrology

Indicator status: Obligate wetland

Salinity: brackish to salt water; up to 35 ppt

Tidal zone: upper 50% of the intertidal zone; in sandy soils, up to spring tide elevation

Nontidal regime:

Spartina cynosuroides
Big cordgrass, Salt reed grass

Characteristics
Herbaceous / Perennial / Persistent

GROWTH
Rate of spread: moderate; approximately 0.5 ft. per yr. in unconsolidated sediment
Method of vegetative reproduction: rhizome

PLANTING
Suggested spacing:

For uniform ground cover	plant at
in 1 yr.	1 ft. OC
in 2 yrs.	2 ft. OC
in 3 yrs.	3 ft. OC

Forms available: bare root plant, peat pot

HABITAT
Community: fresh and brackish tidal marshes

Distribution: Massachusetts south to Florida and Texas

Shade: requires full sun

NOTES
Soil stabilizer

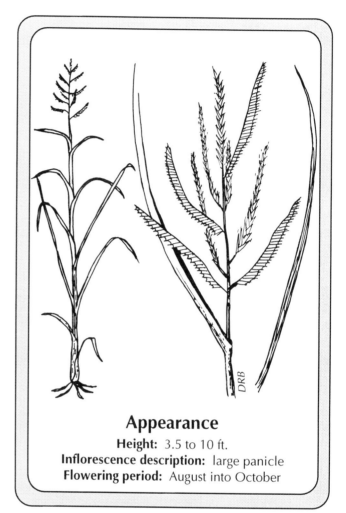

Appearance
Height: 3.5 to 10 ft.
Inflorescence description: large panicle
Flowering period: August into October

Wildlife Benefits
Potential Benefits and Species Served

Food (seeds, rootstocks): black duck, Canada and snow geese, rails, seaside and sharp-tailed sparrows, muskrat

Hydrology

Indicator status: Obligate wetland

Salinity: fresh to brackish water; up to approximately 10 ppt

Tidal zone: near mean high water and above to spring tide elevation

Nontidal regime:

Spartina patens
Salt marsh hay, Saltmeadow cordgrass, Highwater grass

Characteristics

Herbaceous / Perennial / Semi-persistent

GROWTH
Rate of spread: moderate; approximately 0.5 ft. per yr. in unconsolidated sediment
Method of vegetative reproduction: rhizome

PLANTING
Suggested spacing:

For uniform ground cover	plant at
in 1 yr.	1 ft. OC
in 2 yrs.	2 ft. OC
in 3 yrs.	3 ft. OC

Forms available: bare root plant, peat pot, container

HABITAT
Community: brackish and salt marshes

Distribution: southwestern Newfoundland to southern St. Lawrence, Quebec, south to Florida and Texas, inland to western New York and southeastern Michigan

Shade: requires full sun

NOTES
Soil stabilizer
pH preference = 3.7 - 7.9
Tolerates drought

Appearance
Leans over in large monotypic stands
Height: 1 to 3 ft.
Flowering period: late June into October

Wildlife Benefits
Potential Benefits and Species Served

Food (rootstocks, seeds): Canada and snow geese, black duck, sparrows, rails

Hydrology

Indicator status: Facultative wetland +

Salinity: brackish to salt water; up to 35 ppt

Tidal zone: near mean high water and above to upland

Nontidal regime:

Spartina pectinata
Prairie cordgrass

Characteristics
Herbaceous / Perennial

GROWTH
Rate of spread: moderate; approximately 0.5 ft. per yr. in unconsolidated sediment
Method of vegetative reproduction: rhizome

PLANTING
Suggested spacing:

For uniform ground cover	plant at
in 1 yr.	1 ft. OC
in 2 yrs.	2 ft. OC
in 3 yrs.	3 ft. OC

Forms available: seed, rhizome, bare root plant

HABITAT
Community: brackish and fresh tidal marshes
nontidal marshes
shores
wet meadows

Distribution: Newfoundland to Alberta and Washington south to Nova Scotia, New England, western North Carolina, West Virginia, Indiana, Illinois, Missouri, Texas, New Mexico, Oregon

Shade: requires full sun

NOTES
Good for shore stabilization

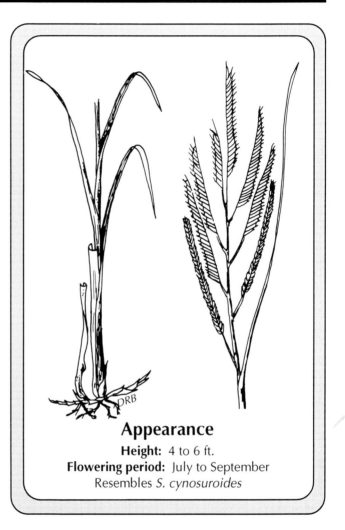

Appearance
Height: 4 to 6 ft.
Flowering period: July to September
Resembles *S. cynosuroides*

Wildlife Benefits
Potential Benefits and Species Served

Food (rootstocks, seed, plants): waterfowl (black duck), marshbirds, shorebirds, songbirds, aquatic furbearers, deer

Nesting: marsh wren

Habitat: muskrat

Hydrology

Indicator status: Obligate wetland

Salinity: fresh to brackish water; up to approximately 3 ppt

Tidal zone: upper 50% of the intertidal zone and above to spring tide elevation

Nontidal regime: regularly to permanently inundated up to 0.5 ft. or saturated (approximately 26 to 100% of the growing season)

Symplocarpus foetidus
Skunk cabbage

Characteristics
Herbaceous / Perennial / Nonpersistent

GROWTH
Rate of spread: slow; less than 0.2 ft. per yr. in unconsolidated sediment
Method of vegetative reproduction: rhizome

PLANTING
Suggested spacing: in clusters

For uniform aerial cover	plant at
in 1 yr.	0.5 ft. OC
in 2 yrs.	1.0 ft. OC
in 3 yrs.	1.5 ft. OC

Forms available: bare root plant

HABITAT
Community: fresh tidal marshes and swamps
nontidal marshes
shrub swamps
forested wetlands
seeps

Distribution: Quebec to southeastern Manitoba, south to North Carolina and Iowa, upland to Georgia and Tennessee

Shade: tolerates full shade

NOTES

Appearance
Height: leaves up to 2 ft.
Flower description: purple and green variegated spathe (hoodlike structure) surrounds a spadix (spike bearing inconspicuous flowers)
Flowering period: February into May (flowers emerge before leaves)

Wildlife Benefits
Potential Benefits and Species Served

Food (fruit, leaves): upland gamebirds (ring-necked pheasant)

Hydrology

Indicator status: Obligate wetland

Salinity: fresh water; less than 0.5 ppt

Tidal zone:

Nontidal regime: seasonally, regularly, or permanently saturated (approximately 13 to 100% of the growing season)

Thelypteris noveboracensis
New York fern

Characteristics

Herbaceous / Perennial / Nonpersistent

GROWTH
Rate of spread:
Method of vegetative reproduction: rhizome

PLANTING
Suggested spacing:
Forms available: container

HABITAT
Community: forested wetlands

Distribution: Newfoundland to southern Ontario, Michigan and northern Illinois, south to Nova Scotia, New England, Georgia, Alabama, Michigan, and Arkansas

Shade: tolerates full shade

NOTES
Tolerates drought
Grows in tufts, but may cover considerable area

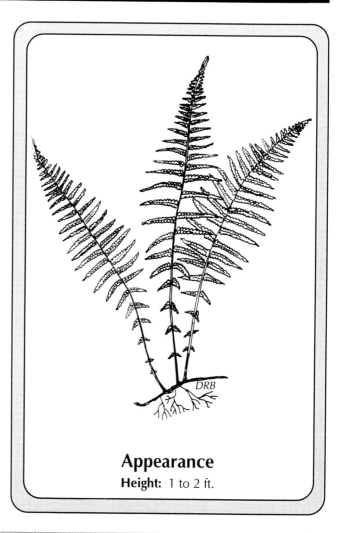

Appearance
Height: 1 to 2 ft.

Wildlife Benefits

Potential Benefits and Species Served

Food (leaves): upland gamebirds, mammals (e.g., snowshoe hare, deer)

Hydrology

Indicator status: Facultative

Salinity: fresh water; less than 0.5 ppt

Tidal zone:

Nontidal regime: irregularly, seasonally, or regularly saturated (up to approximately 75% of the growing season)

Thelypteris palustris
Marsh fern, Meadow fern, Snuffbox fern

Characteristics
Herbaceous / Perennial / Nonpersistent

GROWTH
Rate of spread: moderate; approximately 0.5 ft. per yr. in unconsolidated sediment
Method of vegetative reproduction: rhizome

PLANTING
Suggested spacing:

For uniform ground cover	plant at
in 1 yr.	1 ft. OC
in 2 yrs.	2 ft. OC
in 3 yrs.	3 ft. OC

Forms available: plug, container

HABITAT
Community: fresh tidal marshes
            nontidal marshes
            shrub swamps
            forested wetlands
            wooded stream banks

Distribution: southern Newfoundland to southeastern Manitoba, south to Florida and Texas

Shade: tolerates full shade

NOTES
Prefers fertile, acidic soil

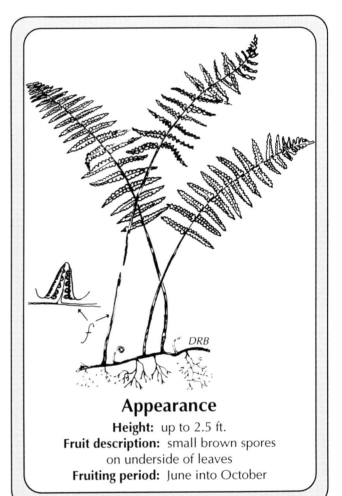

Appearance
Height: up to 2.5 ft.
Fruit description: small brown spores on underside of leaves
Fruiting period: June into October

Wildlife Benefits
Potential Benefits and Species Served

Food (leaves): upland gamebirds, mammals (e.g., snowshoe hare, deer)

Hydrology

Indicator status: Facultative wetland +

Salinity: fresh; less than 0.5 ppt

Tidal zone: near mean high water and above to spring tide elevation

Nontidal regime: irregularly, seasonally, regularly, or permanently saturated (up to 100% of the growing season)

Typha angustifolia
Narrow-leaved cattail

Characteristics
Herbaceous / Perennial / Persistent

GROWTH
Rate of spread: rapid; over 1 ft. per yr. in unconsolidated sediment
Method of vegetative reproduction: rhizome

PLANTING
Suggested spacing:

For uniform ground cover	plant at
in 1 yr.	2 ft. OC
in 2 yrs.	4 ft. OC
in 3 yrs.	6 ft. OC

Forms available: dormant rhizome, bare root plant, peat pot, container

HABITAT
Community: fresh and brackish tidal marshes; nontidal marshes; pond and stream edges

Distribution: Nova Scotia and southern Maine to southern Quebec and Ontario south to Florida and Texas, Kentucky, Missouri, Nebraska, and California

Shade: requires full sun

NOTES
Soil stabilizer
pH range = 3.7 - 8.5
Tolerates drought
This species distinguished from *T. latifolia* by its **tolerance** for moderate salinity and **separation** between male and female spikes

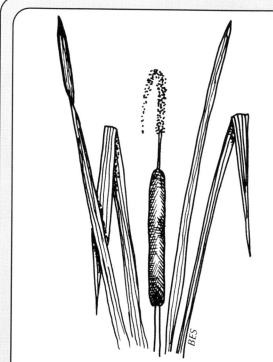

Appearance
Height: up to 10 ft.
Flower description: inconspicuous in large, dense, brown terminal spike; male spike above and **separate from** female spike
Flowering period: June to July

Wildlife Benefits
Potential Benefits and Species Served

Food (seeds, rootsocks): snow goose, teals, muskrat, beaver

Cover, Nesting: canvasback, gadwall, wood duck, marsh wren, red-winged blackbird, young fish

Spawning grounds: sunfish

Hydrology

Indicator status: Obligate wetland

Salinity: fresh to brackish water; up to 15 ppt

Tidal zone: upper 20% of the intertidal zone to spring tide elevation

Nontidal regime: irregularly, seasonally, regularly, or permanently inundated up to 1 ft. or saturated (up to approximately 100% of the growing season)

Typha latifolia
Broad-leaved cattail

**CAUTION:
Possibly Invasive**

Characteristics
Herbaceous / Perennial / Persistent

GROWTH
Rate of spread: rapid; over 1 ft. per yr. in unconsolidated sediment
Method of vegetative reproduction: rhizome

PLANTING
Suggested spacing:

For uniform ground cover	plant at
in 1 yr.	2 ft. OC
in 2 yrs.	4 ft. OC
in 3 yrs.	6 ft. OC

Forms available: dormant rhizome, bare root plant, peat pot, container

HABITAT
Community: fresh tidal marshes
nontidal marshes
pond and stream edges
ditches

Distribution: Newfoundland to Alaska, south to Florida and Mexico

Shade: requires full sun

NOTES
Soil stabilizer
Tolerates drought
May have allelopathic characteristics
This species distinguished from *T. angustifolia* by its **lack** of tolerance of salinity and by male and female spikes with no space between them

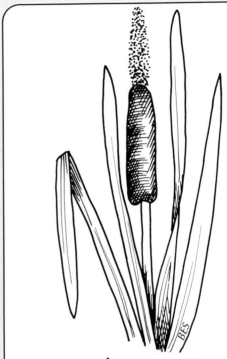

Appearance
Height: up to 10 ft.
Flower description: inconspicuous in large, dense, brown terminal spike; male spike above and **touching** female spike
Flowering period: May into June

Wildlife Benefits
Potential Benefits and Species Served

Food (seeds, rootsocks): snow goose, teals, muskrat, beaver

Cover, Nesting: canvasback, gadwall, wood duck, marsh wren, red-winged blackbird, fish

Hydrology

Indicator status: Obligate wetland

Salinity: fresh water; less than 0.5 ppt

Tidal zone: upper 20% of the intertidal zone to spring tide elevation

Nontidal regime: irregularly, seasonally, regularly, or permanently inundated up to 1 ft. or saturated (up to approximately 100% of the growing season)

Woodwardia areolata
Netted chain fern

Characteristics
Herbaceous / Perennial / Nonpersistent

GROWTH
Rate of spread:
Method of vegetative reproduction:

PLANTING
Suggested spacing:
Forms available: container

HABITAT
Community: forested wetlands
shrub wetlands
bogs
seepage slopes

Distribution: Nova Scotia south to Florida and Texas
(mainly along coast), west to Michigan and Missouri

Shade: tolerates full shade

NOTES
Prefers moderately or highly acidic soils

Appearance
Height: up to 4 ft.
Fruiting period: July through September

Wildlife Benefits
Potential Benefits and Species Served

Food (leaves): upland gamebirds, mammals (e.g., snowshoe hare, deer)

Hydrology

Indicator status: Facultative wetland +

Salinity: fresh water; less than 0.5 ppt

Tidal zone:

Nontidal regime: irregularly, seasonally, regularly, or permanently saturated (up to approximately 100% of the growing season)

Zizania aquatica
Wild rice

Characteristics
Herbaceous / Annual / Nonpersistent

GROWTH
Rate of spread:
Method of vegetative reproduction: none

PLANTING
Suggested spacing:
Forms available: seed, peat pot

HABITAT
Community: fresh tidal marshes
nontidal marshes
stream borders
shallow waters

Distribution: eastern Quebec and Nova Scotia to Manitoba, south to Florida and Louisiana (varieties occur across this range)

Shade: requires full sun

NOTES

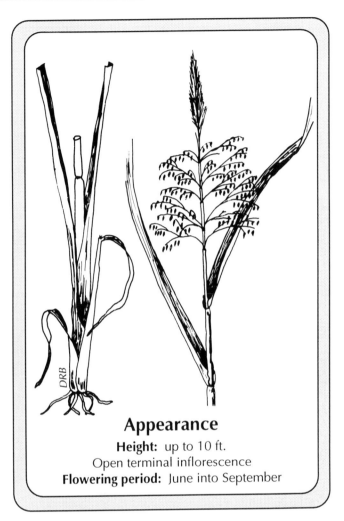

Appearance
Height: up to 10 ft.
Open terminal inflorescence
Flowering period: June into September

Wildlife Benefits
Potential Benefits and Species Served

Food (seeds, plant parts, rootstocks): wood duck, black duck, other waterfowl, red-winged blackbird, rail, bobolink, muskrat

Hydrology

Indicator status: Obligate wetland

Salinity: resistant; tolerates infrequent flooding by water containing some salt

Tidal zone: middle 50% of the intertidal zone

Nontidal regime: regularly to permanently inundated up to 3 ft. (in clear water) or saturated (approximately 26 to 100% of the growing season)

PLANT SHEETS

Shrubs

Alnus serrulata
Smooth alder, Hazel alder, Tag alder

Characteristics
Broad-leaved, deciduous shrub

GROWTH
Rate: fast; 2 ft. per yr.

PLANTING
Forms available: container

HABITAT
Community: fresh tidal marshes
nontidal marshes
shrub swamps and forested wetlands

Distribution: Nova Scotia, south to northwestern
Florida, west to Illinois and Oklahoma

Shade: requires full sun

NOTES
Nitrogen fixing
Susceptible to wind or ice damage (weak wooded)
pH tolerance = 5.5 - 7.5

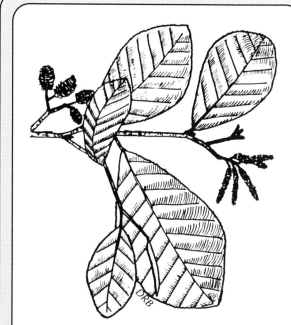

Appearance
Height: 12 to 20 ft.
Aerial spread: 12 to 20 ft.
Flower color: purple (catkins)
Flowering period: mid- through late March
Fruit description: small, brown, cone-like
Fruiting period: early August,
persisting through February

Wildlife Benefits (*Alnus spp.*)
Potential Benefits and Species Served

Food (seeds or buds): pine siskin, American goldfinch,
ruffed grouse, bobwhite, mourning dove, purple
finch, common redpoll, tree sparrow

Food (seeds) and Cover: ducks: mallard, wigeon, green-
winged teal, bufflehead; wild turkey, ring-necked
pheasant, rose-breasted grosbeak

Nesting and/or Cover: American woodcock, willow
flycatcher, alder flycatcher, yellow and Wilson's
warblers, red-winged and rusty blackbirds, rose-
breasted grosbeak, fox and song sparrows,
beaver (preferred)

Hydrology

Indicator status: Obligate wetland

Salinity: fresh water; less than 0.5 ppt

Tidal zone: above mean high water to upland

Nontidal regime: seasonally to regularly inundated
up to 3 in. or saturated (approximately 13 to
75% of the growing season)

Amorpha fruticosa
False indigo bush, Indigo bush

Characteristics
Broad-leaved, deciduous shrub

GROWTH
Rate: medium; 1 to 2 ft. per yr

PLANTING
Forms available: bare root

HABITAT
Community: shrub swamps
forested wetlands

Distribution: New England to Minnesota and Saskatchewan, south to Florida and Texas (varieties occur across this range)

Shade: requires full sun

NOTES
Susceptible to wind or ice damage (weak wooded)
pH preference = 6.0 - 8.5
Tolerates drought
Soil stabilizer

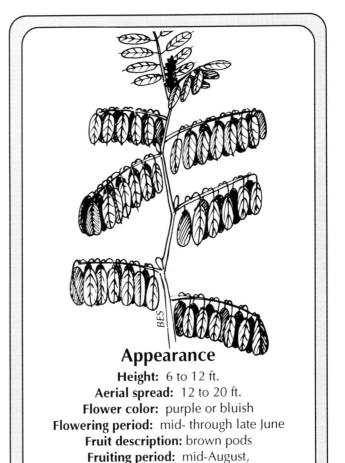

Appearance
Height: 6 to 12 ft.
Aerial spread: 12 to 20 ft.
Flower color: purple or bluish
Flowering period: mid- through late June
Fruit description: brown pods
Fruiting period: mid-August,
persisting to late March

Wildlife Benefits
Potential Benefits and Species Served

Food and Cover: bobwhite, waterfowl, marshbirds, shorebirds, small mammals

Hydrology

Indicator status: Facultative wetland

Salinity: resistant; tolerates infrequent flooding by water containing some salt

Tidal zone: above spring tide elevation

Nontidal regime: irregularly to seasonally inundated or saturated (up to approximately 25% of the growing season)

Environmental Concern Inc.

Aronia arbutifolia (Pyrus arbutifolia)
Red chokeberry

Characteristics
Broad-leaved, deciduous shrub

GROWTH
Rate: slow; 1ft. or less per yr.
Spreads by suckers

PLANTING
Forms available: rooted cutting, container, balled and
burlapped

HABITAT
Community: forested seasonal wetlands
shrub bogs;
sometimes in upland soil

Distribution: Nova Scotia and Michigan to Florida and
Texas

Shade: tolerates partial shade

NOTES
pH preference = 5.0 - 6.5
Tolerates drought

Appearance
Height: 6 to 12 ft.
Aerial spread: 3 to 6 ft.
Flower color: white
Flowering period: mid- through late May
Fruit color: red
Fruiting period: early September through
mid-December

Wildlife Benefits
Potential Benefits and Species Served

Food (fruit): bobwhite, brown thrasher, cedar waxwing,
eastern meadowlark, fur and game mammals, small
and hoofed mammals

Also serves as emergency food in winter to many species

Hydrology

Indicator status: Facultative wetland

Salinity: resistant; tolerates infrequent flooding by
water containing some salt

Tidal zone: above spring tide elevation

Nontidal regime: irregularly to seasonally inundated
or saturated (up to approximately 25% of the
growing season)

Aronia melanocarpa *(Pyrus melanocarpa)*
Black chokeberry

Characteristics
Broad-leaved, deciduous shrub

GROWTH
Rate: slow; less than 1 ft. per yr.
Spreads by suckers

PLANTING
Forms available: plug, container

HABITAT
Community: swamp and bog edges
clearings

Distribution: Newfoundland to northwestern Ontario
and Minnesota, south to Nova Scotia, New England,
South Carolina, and Tennessee

Shade: tolerates partial shade

NOTES
Relatively insensitive to disease, insect, and wind or ice
damage
pH preference = 5.1 - 6.5
Tolerates drought

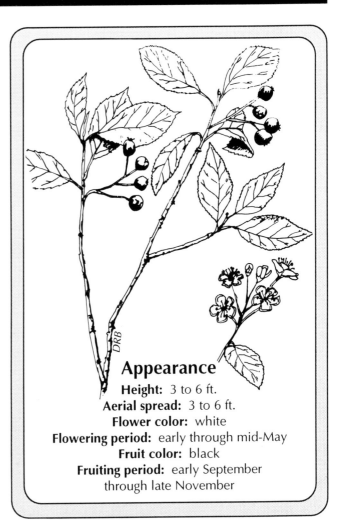

Appearance
Height: 3 to 6 ft.
Aerial spread: 3 to 6 ft.
Flower color: white
Flowering period: early through mid-May
Fruit color: black
Fruiting period: early September
through late November

Wildlife Benefits
Potential Benefits and Species Served

Food (fruit): black-capped chickadee, bobwhite, gray
catbird, brown thrasher, cedar waxwing, eastern
meadowlark, large and small mammals

Food (fruit, buds): ruffed grouse

Food (twigs, foliage, fruit): hoofed browsers

Hydrology

Indicator status: Facultative

Salinity: resistant; tolerates infrequent flooding by
water containing some salt

Tidal zone:

Nontidal regime: irregularly to seasonally saturated
(up to approximately 25% of the growing
season)

Environmental Concern Inc.

Baccharis halimifolia
Groundsel tree, Sea myrtle, Eastern false willow, Consumption weed

Characteristics
Broad-leaved, deciduous shrub

GROWTH
Rate: fast; 2 ft. or more per yr.

PLANTING
Forms available: container

HABITAT
Community: salt or brackish marshes
fresh tidal marshes

Distribution: coastal Massachusetts, south to Florida, Texas and Mexico

Shade: requires full sun

NOTES
pH preference = 7.0 - 8.5
Male and female flowers on separate plants

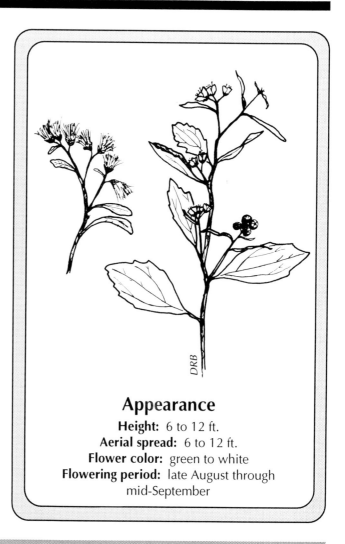

Appearance
Height: 6 to 12 ft.
Aerial spread: 6 to 12 ft.
Flower color: green to white
Flowering period: late August through mid-September

Wildlife Benefits
Potential Benefits and Species Served

Very low value for wildlife

Cover, Nesting, Breeding: some songbirds

Hydrology

Indicator status: Facultative wetland

Salinity: brackish to salt water

Tidal zone: above mean high water to upland

Nontidal regime: seasonally to regularly inundated up to 0.5 ft. or saturated (approximately 13 to 75% of the growing season)

Cephalanthus occidentalis
Buttonbush

Characteristics
Broad-leaved, deciduous shrub

GROWTH
Rate: medium; 1 to 2 ft. per yr.

PLANTING
Forms available: seedling, plug, bare root, unrooted and rooted cuttings, container

HABITAT
Community: fresh tidal marshes
nontidal marshes
shrub swamps
forested wetlands
borders of streams, lakes, and ponds

Distribution: New Brunswick and Quebec to Minnesota, south to Florida, Mexico, and California

Shade: tolerates full shade; flowers best in partial shade and full sun

NOTES
Roots readily from cuttings
Tolerates wide range of conditions, including drought
Fairly insensitive to disease, insect, and wind or ice damage
pH preference = 6.0 - 8.5

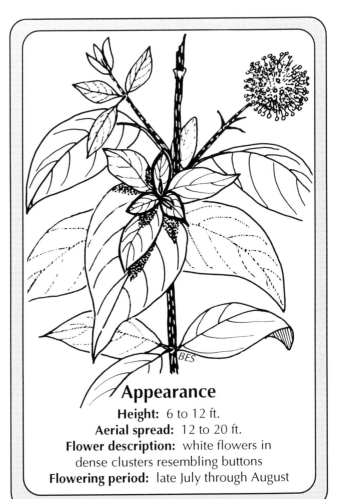

Appearance
Height: 6 to 12 ft.
Aerial spread: 12 to 20 ft.
Flower description: white flowers in dense clusters resembling buttons
Flowering period: late July through August

Wildlife Benefits
Potential Benefits and Species Served

Food (nutlet): ducks: mallard, wigeon, shoveler, wood, and teals

Food (twigs, foliage): deer

Food (nectar): ruby-throated hummingbird

Nesting: Virginia rail, red-winged blackbird

Attracts: muskrat, beaver

Hydrology

Indicator status: Obligate wetland

Salinity: resistant; tolerates infrequent flooding by water containing some salt

Tidal zone: near mean high water and above to upland

Nontidal regime: irregularly to permanently inundated up to 3 ft. or saturated (up to 100% of the growing season)

Clethra alnifolia
Sweet pepperbush

Characteristics
Broad-leaved, deciduous shrub

GROWTH
Rate: slow; less than 1 ft. per yr.
Spreads by suckers

PLANTING
Forms available: bare root plant, container

HABITAT
Community: tidal and nontidal forested wetlands
shrub swamps
sandy woods
coastal river floodplains

Distribution: southern Maine, south to Florida and
eastern Texas

Shade: tolerates full shade; flowers best in partial shade
and full sun

NOTES
pH preference = 4.5 - 6.5
Fairly insensitive to disease, insect, and wind or ice
damage
Susceptible to red mites, especially under drier conditions

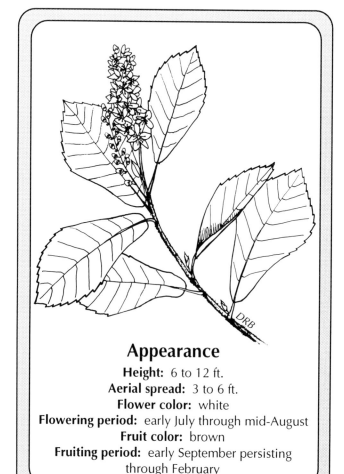

Appearance
Height: 6 to 12 ft.
Aerial spread: 3 to 6 ft.
Flower color: white
Flowering period: early July through mid-August
Fruit color: brown
Fruiting period: early September persisting
through February

Wildlife Benefits
Potential Benefits and Species Served

Food and Cover: songbirds, shorebirds, waterfowl,
upland gamebirds, small mammals

Hydrology

Indicator status: Facultative +

Salinity: resistant; tolerates infrequent flooding by
water containing some salt

Tidal zone: near mean high water and above to
spring tide elevation

Nontidal regime: seasonally to regularly inundated
or saturated (tolerates frequent temporary
inundation for approximately 13 to 75% of the
growing season)

Cornus amomum
Silky dogwood

Characteristics
Broad-leaved, deciduous shrub

GROWTH
Rate: fast; 2 ft. or more per yr.

PLANTING
Forms available: rooted cutting, container, balled and
burlapped

HABITAT
Community: forested seasonal wetlands
shrub wetlands
stream and pond banks
moist woods

Distribution: Quebec to Ontario and southern Illinois,
south to South Carolina and Alabama

Shade: prefers full sun, tolerates partial shade

NOTES
Fairly insensitive to insect and wind or ice damage
pH preference = 5.5 - 7.5 (tolerates 8.5)
Tolerates drought
Transplants well

Appearance
Height: 6 to 12 ft.
Aerial spread: 6 to 12 ft.
Flower color: yellowish white
Flowering period: May through July
Fruit color: blue
Fruiting period: early through late August

Wildlife Benefits
Potential Benefits and Species Served

Food (fruit, twigs, or leaves): wild turkey, ruffed grouse,
bobwhite, ring-necked pheasant, common flicker;
red-headed, downy, and pileated woodpeckers;
eastern kingbird, brown thrasher, American robin,
wood and Swainson's thrushes, eastern bluebird,
cedar waxwing, purple finch, white-tailed deer,
beaver, cottontail rabbit, woodchuck, raccoon,
squirrel

Cover and Food: wood duck, American woodcock,
song sparrow

Preferred Nesting, Cover, and Food: gray catbird

Nesting and Cover: American goldfinch

Hydrology

Indicator status: Facultative wetland

Salinity: fresh water; less than 0.5 ppt

Tidal zone: above spring tide elevation

Nontidal regime: irregularly to seasonally inundated
or saturated (up to approximately 25% of the
growing season)

Cornus foemina racemosa (C. racemosa, C. stricta)
Graystem dogwood

Characteristics
Broad-leaved, deciduous shrub

GROWTH
Rate: medium; young shoots grow 3 to 6 ft. in one season

PLANTING
Forms available: bare root plant, plug, container

HABITAT
Community: forested wetlands
shrub swamps
stream borders

Distribution: central Maine to southern Ontario and Minnesota, south to New England, Delaware, Maryland, West Virginia, Kentucky, Missouri, and Oklahoma

Shade: tolerates full shade

NOTES
pH tolerance = 5.5 - 8.5
Fairly insensitive to disease, insect, and wind or ice damage
Tolerates drought
May control soil erosion
Tolerates various soil textures
Easily propagated from cuttings

Appearance
Height: 6 to 12 ft.
Aerial spread: 6 to 12 ft.
Flower color: white
Flowering period: late May through mid-June
Fruit color: white
Fruiting period: early August through late September

Wildlife Benefits
Potential Benefits and Species Served

Food (fruit): ruffed and sharp-tailed grouse, bobwhite, wild turkey, pheasant, common flicker, Swainson's thrush, eastern bluebird, cedar waxwing, waterfowl

Food (twigs, foliage): white-tailed deer, beaver, ring-necked pheasant, cottontail rabbit, woodchuck, raccoon, squirrel

Cover: American woodcock

Hydrology

Indicator status: Facultative

Salinity: fresh water; less than 0.5 ppt

Tidal zone:

Nontidal regime: irregularly to seasonally inundated or saturated (up to approximately 25% of the growing season)

Cornus sericea (C. stolonifera)
Red-osier dogwood

Characteristics
Broad-leaved, deciduous shrub

GROWTH
Rate: fast; 2 ft. or more per yr.
Spreads by stolons

PLANTING
Forms available: seed, bare root plant, container, balled
and burlapped

HABITAT
Community: forested seasonal wetlands
shrub wetlands
stream banks

Distribution: Newfoundland and southern Labrador to
Yukon Territory, south to Nova Scotia, New Eng-
land, West Virginia, Ohio, Indiana, Illinois, Iowa,
Nebraska, New Mexico, Arizona, and California

Shade: tolerates partial shade

NOTES
pH tolerance = 5.5 - 8.5
Fairly insensitive to wind or ice damage
Tolerates drought
Used in streambank stabilization
Easily propagated from cuttings

Appearance
Height: 6 to 12 ft.
Aerial spread: 6 to 12 ft.
Flower color: white
Flowering period: late May through mid-June
Fruit color: white
Fruiting period: September

Wildlife Benefits
Potential Benefits and Species Served

Food: eastern kingbird, brown thrasher, ring-necked
pheasant, white-tailed deer and other hoofed
browsers, wild turkey, beaver, ruffed and sharp-
tailed grouse, bobwhite, cottontail rabbit, snowshoe
hare, woodchuck, raccoon, moose

Cover and Nesting: American goldfinch

Hydrology

Indicator status: Facultative wetland +

Salinity: fresh water; less than 0.5 ppt

Tidal zone:

Nontidal regime: irregularly to seasonally inundated
or saturated (up to approximately 25% of the
growing season)

Ilex decidua

Possumhaw, Deciduous holly

Characteristics

Broad-leaved, deciduous shrub

GROWTH
Rate: slow to medium; 1 to 2 ft. per yr.

PLANTING
Forms available: container

HABITAT
Community: swamps
                  pond edges
                  floodplain forests

Distribution: Coastal Plain, Maryland to Florida and Texas, eastern Oklahoma, north to southern Indiana, southern Illinois, southern Missouri, and Kansas

Shade: tolerates full shade

NOTES
Fairly insensitive to disease, insect, and wind or ice damage
pH preference = 4.0 - 6.0 (tolerates 8.5)
Tolerates drought
Male and female flowers on separate plants (Note: *Ilex* species can pollinate other species of *Ilex*)

Appearance
BES
Height: 12 to 20 ft.
Aerial spread: 12 to 20 ft.
Flower color: green to white
Flowering period: late May through mid-June
Fruit color: orange to red
Fruiting period: after first frost in October, persists to late March

Wildlife Benefits (*Ilex spp.*)

Potential Benefits and Species Served

Food (fruit): black and wood ducks, wild turkey, ruffed grouse, bobwhite, ring-necked pheasant, mourning dove, common flicker, pileated and red-bellied woodpeckers, yellow-bellied sapsucker, eastern phoebe, American crow, gray catbird, brown thrasher; wood, hermit, Swainson's , and gray-cheeked thrushes; eastern bluebird, cedar waxwing, white-eyed vireo, cardinal, purple finch, rufous-sided towhee, white-throated sparrow

Food (fruit), Cover, Nesting: mockingbird, American robin, veery

Food (new growth): Deer

Hydrology

Indicator status: Facultative wetland

Salinity: resistant; tolerates infrequent flooding by water containing some salt

Tidal zone:

Nontidal regime: irregularly to seasonally inundated or saturated (up to approximately 25% of the growing season)

Ilex glabra
Bitter gallberry, Inkberry

Characteristics
Broad-leaved, evergreen shrub

GROWTH
Rate: slow; up to 1 ft. per yr.

PLANTING
Forms available: seed, container, balled and burlapped

HABITAT
Community: forested seasonal wetlands
shrub swamps
sandy woods

Distribution: Nova Scotia to Florida and Louisiana (along Coastal Plain)

Shade: tolerates partial shade

NOTES
Fairly insensitive to disease and insect damage
pH preference = 4.5 - 6.0
Male and female flowers on separate plants (Note: *Ilex* species can pollinate other species of *Ilex*)

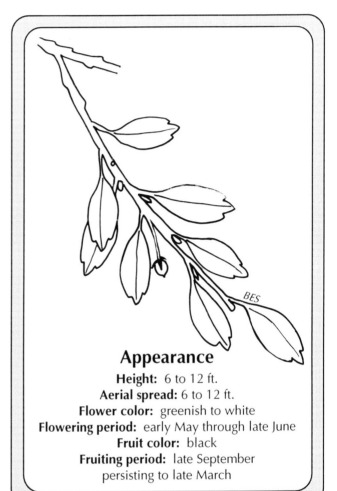

Appearance
Height: 6 to 12 ft.
Aerial spread: 6 to 12 ft.
Flower color: greenish to white
Flowering period: early May through late June
Fruit color: black
Fruiting period: late September persisting to late March

Wildlife Benefits
Potential Benefits and Species Served

Food (fruit): wild turkey, bobwhite, common flicker, hermit thrush, eastern bluebird, cedar waxwing, rufous-sided towhee, waterfowl, large and small mammals

Food (fruit), Cover, Nesting: mockingbird, American robin

Hydrology

Indicator status: Facultative wetland –

Salinity: resistant; tolerates infrequent flooding by water containing some salt; tolerates salt spray

Tidal zone:

Nontidal regime: seasonally inundated or saturated (approximately 13 to 26% of the growing season)

Environmental Concern Inc.

Ilex verticillata
Common winterberry, Winterberry holly, Black alder, Swamp holly

Characteristics
Broad-leaved, deciduous shrub

GROWTH
Rate: slow; 1 ft. or less per yr.

PLANTING
Forms available: seed, rooted cutting, container, balled and burlapped

HABITAT
Community: fresh tidal swamps
shrub swamps
forested wetlands

Distribution: Newfoundland to Minnesota, south to Georgia and Mississippi

Shade: prefers at least partial shade, tolerates full shade

NOTES
Male and female flowers on different plants (Note: *Ilex* species can pollinate other species of *Ilex*)
Fairly insensitive to disease, insect, and wind or ice damage
pH preference = 4.5 to 6.0 (tolerates up to 8.0)
Tolerates drought

Appearance
Height: 6 to 12 ft.
Aerial spread: 6 to 12 ft.
Flower color: greenish to white
Flowering period: early through late June
Fruit color: red to orange
Fruiting season: late August persisting through February

Wildlife Benefits
Potential Benefits and Species Served

Important for emergency food in winter

Food (berries, other): mockingbird, gray catbird, brown thrasher, hermit thrush, black duck, bobwhite, common flicker, American crow, American robin, cedar waxwing, cottontail rabbit, raccoon, white-footed mouse, squirrel, ruffed grouse, ring-necked pheasant, eastern bluebird, raccoon, deer

Food, Cover, Nesting: veery, red-winged blackbird

Hydrology

Indicator status: Facultative wetland +

Salinity: fresh water; less than 0.5 ppt

Tidal zone: above mean high water to upland

Nontidal regime: irregularly to seasonally inundated or saturated (up to approximately 25% of the growing season)

Itea virginica
Tassel-white, Virginia sweetspire

Characteristics
Broad-leaved, deciduous shrub

GROWTH
Rate: slow to medium; 1 to 2 ft. per yr.

PLANTING
Forms available: container

HABITAT
Community: forested wetlands
shrub swamps
stream banks

Distribution: southern New Jersey, south to Florida and Louisiana (along Coastal Plain), Mississippi Valley, north to Illinois

Shade: tolerates full shade

NOTES
Fairly insensitive to disease, insect, and wind or ice damage
pH preference = 5.0 - 7.0

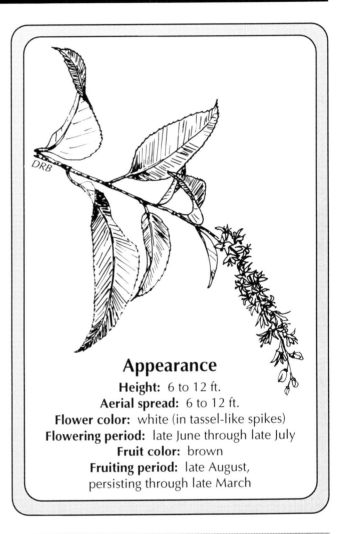

Appearance
Height: 6 to 12 ft.
Aerial spread: 6 to 12 ft.
Flower color: white (in tassel-like spikes)
Flowering period: late June through late July
Fruit color: brown
Fruiting period: late August, persisting through late March

Wildlife Benefits
Potential Benefits and Species Served

Low wildlife value

Food, Cover: waterbirds, songbirds, gamebirds, small mammals

Hydrology

Indicator status: Obligate wetland

Salinity: resistant; tolerates infrequent flooding by water containing some salt

Tidal zone:

Nontidal regime: seasonally, regularly, or permanently inundated up to 0.5 ft. or saturated (approximately 13 to 100% of the growing season)

Iva frutescens

Marsh elder, High tide bush

Characteristics
Broad-leaved, deciduous shrub

GROWTH
Rate: slow; less than 1 ft. per yr.

PLANTING
Forms available: container

HABITAT
Community: tidal brackish and salt marshes

Distribution: Nova Scotia and southern New Hampshire, south to Florida and Texas

Shade: requires full sun

NOTES
pH preference = 6.0 - 7.5

Appearance
Height: 2 to 10 ft.
Flower color: greenish white (in spikes)
Flowering period: August through October

Wildlife Benefits
Potential Benefits and Species Served

Low wildlife value

Cover, Nesting, Breeding: red-winged blackbird, roseate spoonbill

Hydrology

Indicator status: Facultative wetland +

Salinity: brackish to salt water

Tidal zone: near mean high water and above to upland

Nontidal regime:

Leucothoe racemosa
Fetterbush

Characteristics
Broad-leaved, deciduous shrub

GROWTH
Rate:

PLANTING
Forms available: container

HABITAT
Community: shrub swamps
forested wetlands
moist acid woods

Distribution: Massachusetts and southeastern New York
to eastern Pennsylvania, south to Florida and
Louisiana

Shade: tolerates full shade

NOTES
pH preference = 5.0 - 6.0

Appearance
Height: up to 13 ft.
Flower color: white
Flowering period: May to June
(buds develop during previous summer)

Wildlife Benefits
Potential Benefits and Species Served

Food: white-tailed deer

Hydrology

Indicator status: Facultative wetland

Salinity: fresh water; less than 0.5 ppt

Tidal zone:

Nontidal regime: seasonally to regularly inundated
or saturated (approximately 13 to 75% of
growing season with dry-down occurring at
intervals during this period)

Lindera benzoin (Benzoin aestivale)
Common spicebush

Characteristics
Broad-leaved, deciduous shrub

GROWTH
Rate: slow; 1 ft. per yr. or less

PLANTING
Forms available: container, balled and burlapped

HABITAT
Community: forested seasonal wetlands
moist upland woods
floodplains

Distribution: southwestern Maine to southern Ontario, southern Michigan and Illinois, south to Florida and Texas

Shade: tolerates full shade

NOTES
Fairly insensitive to disease, insect, and wind or ice damage
pH preference = 4.5 - 6.5
Male and female flowers are on separate plants
Tolerates drought

BES

Appearance
Height: 6 to 12 ft.
Aerial spread: 6 to 12 ft.
Flower color: greenish yellow
Flowering period: early through late April
Fruit color: red
Fruiting period: early through late September

Wildlife Benefits
Potential Benefits and Species Served

Food: veery, ruffed grouse, bobwhite, ring-necked pheasant, common flicker, eastern kingbird, great-crested flycatcher, gray catbird, American robin, cardinal, white-throated sparrow, wild turkey, red-eyed vireo; wood, hermit, and gray-cheeked thrushes

Browsing: white-tailed deer

Hydrology

Indicator status: Facultative wetland –

Salinity: resistant; tolerates infrequent flooding by water containing some salt

Tidal zone:

Nontidal regime: seasonally inundated or saturated (approximately 13 to 25% of the growing season)

Magnolia virginiana
Sweetbay magnolia

Characteristics
Broad-leaved, semi-evergreen shrub

GROWTH
Rate: medium; 1 to 2 ft. per yr.
Spreads by suckers

PLANTING
Forms available: seed, plug, container, balled and
  burlapped

HABITAT
Community: forested wetlands
    seeps
    stream and pond borders
    moist sandy woods

Distribution: southern New York, south to Florida and
  Texas (along Coastal Plain)

Shade: tolerates full shade; flowers best in partial shade
  and full sun

NOTES
Fairly insensitive to disease, insect, and wind or ice
  damage
pH preference = 4.0 – 6.5
Tolerates drought

Appearance
Height: 12 to 20 ft.
Aerial spread: 12 to 20 ft.
Flower color: white
Flowering period: late May through mid-June
Fruit color: pink to red
Fruiting period: mid-September through
late October

Wildlife Benefits
Potential Benefits and Species Served

Food (seeds): rufous-sided towhee, red-eyed vireo, red-
  cockaded woodpecker, white-tailed deer, gray
  squirrel

Food (roots): beaver

Nesting/Cover

Hydrology

Indicator status: Facultative wetland +

Salinity: resistant; tolerates infrequent flooding by
  water containing some salt

Tidal zone:

Nontidal regime: irregularly to seasonally inundated
  or saturated (up to approximately 25% of the
  growing season)

Myrica cerifera
Wax myrtle, Candleberry

Characteristics
Broad-leaved, evergreen shrub

GROWTH
Rate:
Spreads by suckers

PLANTING
Forms available: seed, plugs, bare root plant, container

HABITAT
Community: tidal fresh and brackish marshes
nontidal marshes
swamps
sandy dune swales
upland hardwood forests

Distribution: southern New Jersey, south to Florida and Texas

Shade:

NOTES
Nitrogen fixing
pH preference = 4.0 - 6.0
Distinguished from *M. pensylvanica* by its more southern range, its height, and the fact that it is an evergreen
Tolerates drought

Appearance
Height: up to 30 ft.
Flower description: linear and oval catkins
Flowering period: March into June
Fruit color: bluish white

Wildlife Benefits
Potential Benefits and Species Served

Food (fruit): tree swallow, meadowlark, catbird, eastern bluebird, yellow-rumped warbler

Hydrology

Indicator status: Facultative

Salinity: fresh to brackish water; up to 10 ppt

Tidal zone: above mean high water to upland

Nontidal regime: regularly inundated (26 to 75% of the growing season)

Myrica pensylvanica
Bayberry

Characteristics
Broad-leaved, deciduous shrub

GROWTH
Rate: medium; 1 to 2 ft. per yr.
Rate of spread: slow
Spreads by suckers

PLANTING
Forms available: seed, bare root, container, balled and burlapped

HABITAT
Community: tidal fresh and brackish marshes and swamps
nontidal marshes and swamps
sand flats and dunes

Distribution: Newfoundland, south to North Carolina (mainly Coastal Plain)

Shade: tolerates partial shade

NOTES
Nitrogen fixing
Male and female flowers usually on separate plants
pH preference = 5.0 - 6.5
Fairly insensitive to disease, insect and wind or ice damage
Tolerates drought

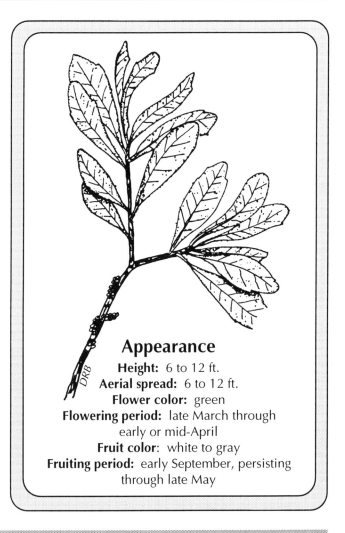

Appearance
Height: 6 to 12 ft.
Aerial spread: 6 to 12 ft.
Flower color: green
Flowering period: late March through early or mid-April
Fruit color: white to gray
Fruiting period: early September, persisting through late May

Wildlife Benefits
Potential Benefits and Species Served

Food: eastern meadowlark, white-eyed vireo, yellow-rumped warbler, tree swallow, red-winged blackbird

Winter food: many songbirds, waterfowl, shorebirds, and marshbirds

Cover: many species

Hydrology

Indicator status: Facultative

Salinity: fresh to brackish water; up to approximately 20 ppt

Tidal zone: above mean high water to upland

Nontidal regime: irregularly to seasonally inundated or saturated (up to approximately 25% of the growing season)

Rhododendron periclymenoides
(R. nudiflorum, Azalea nudiflorum)
Pinxterbloom azalea, Pink azalea, Purple honeysuckle, Election-pink

Characteristics
Broad-leaved deciduous shrub

GROWTH
Rate: slow; less than 1 ft. per yr.
Spreads by stolons

PLANTING
Forms available: container, balled and burlapped

HABITAT
Community: swamp and bog edges
woodlands

Distribution: Massachusetts to New York, west to southern Ohio, south to South Carolina and Tennessee

Shade: tolerates full shade, does not tolerate full sun

NOTES
Demands acid soil, pH = 4.5 - 5.5
Susceptible to leaf spots, crown rot, shoestring root rot, powdery mildew, shoot blight, gray blight, nematodes, rhododendron whitefly, scales, rhododendron tip midge, pitted ambrosia beetle, and others
Fairly insensitive to wind and ice damage

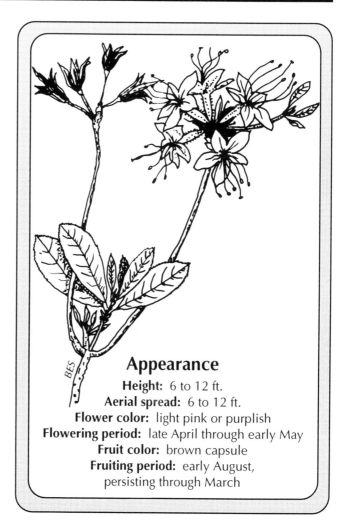

Appearance
Height: 6 to 12 ft.
Aerial spread: 6 to 12 ft.
Flower color: light pink or purplish
Flowering period: late April through early May
Fruit color: brown capsule
Fruiting period: early August, persisting through March

Wildlife Benefits
Potential Benefits and Species Served

Low wildlife value

Food (browsing): deer

Food: upland gamebirds, songbirds, small mammals

Cover

Hydrology

Indicator status: Facultative

Salinity: fresh water; less than 0.5 ppt

Tidal zone:

Nontidal regime: irregularly to seasonally inundated or saturated (up to 25% of the growing season)

Rhododendron viscosum
Swamp azalea

Characteristics
Broad-leaved, deciduous shrub

GROWTH
Rate: slow; 1ft. per yr. or less
Spreads by stolons

PLANTING
Forms available: plug, container

HABITAT
Community: forested wetlands
nontidal swamp edges

Distribution: Maine to Ohio, south to Florida

Shade: tolerates partial shade

NOTES
Highly susceptible to disease and insect damage,
including: Botrytis blotch, bud and twig blight,
Botryosphaera canker, Azalea petal blight, Rhodo-
dendron aphid, Azalea stem borer, Azalea leaf tier,
Strawberry weevil, Azalea leaf minor
Relatively insensitive to wind and ice damage
Demands acid soil; pH = 5.0 - 6.0

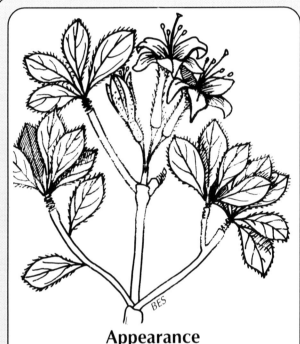

Appearance
Height: 6 to 12 ft.
Aerial spread: 6 to 12 ft.
Flower color: white (pink bud)
Flowering period: early to mid-July
Fruit description: hairy, brown capsules
Fruiting period: early August,
persisting to late March

Wildlife Benefits
Potential Benefits and Species Served

Low wildlife value

Food: waterfowl, marshbirds, shorebirds, small
mammals

Food (browsing): deer

Cover

Hydrology

Indicator status: Obligate wetland

Salinity: fresh water; less than 0.5 ppt

Tidal zone:

Nontidal regime: seasonally to regularly inundated
or saturated (approximately 13 to 75% of the
growing season)

Environmental Concern Inc.

Rosa palustris
Swamp rose

Characteristics
Broad-leaved, deciduous shrub

GROWTH
Rate:

PLANTING
Forms available: container

HABITAT
Community: fresh tidal marshes
nontidal marshes
forested wetlands
shrub swamps
stream banks

Distribution: Nova Scotia and New Brunswick to Minnesota, south to Florida and Arkansas

Shade: prefers full sun

NOTES

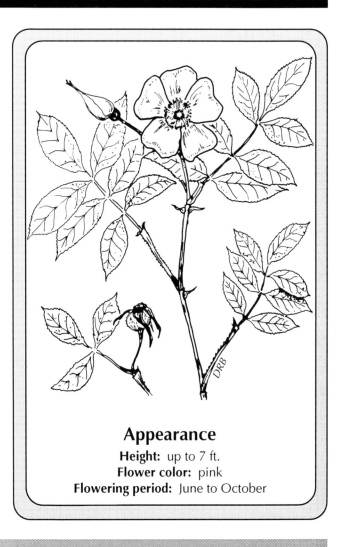

Appearance
Height: up to 7 ft.
Flower color: pink
Flowering period: June to October

Wildlife Benefits
Potential Benefits and Species Served

Food: wild turkey, mockingbird, gray catbird, brown thrasher, American robin, wood and Swainson's thrushes, eastern bluebird, cedar waxwing, white-tailed deer

Food (buds): ruffed grouse, bobwhite, ring-necked pheasant

Cover and Food: cardinal, northern junco; tree, fox, and song sparrows

Hydrology

Indicator status: Obligate wetland

Salinity: fresh water; less than 0.5 ppt

Tidal zone: above spring tide elevation

Nontidal regime: irregularly, seasonally, or regularly saturated (up to approximately 75% of the growing season)

Salix purpurea
Basket willow, Streamco willow, Purpleosier willow

Characteristics
Broad-leaved, deciduous shrub

GROWTH
Rate: fast; up to 2 ft. per yr.
Spreads by suckers

PLANTING
Forms available: bare root

HABITAT
Community: streambanks

Distribution: Newfoundland to Ontario and Wisconsin, south to Nova Scotia, New England, Virginia, West Virginia, Ohio, Illinois, Iowa (varieties occur across this range)

Shade: tolerates partial shade

NOTES
SCS developed *Salix purpurea* 'streamco' specifically for streambank stabilization
Roots readily from cuttings
pH preference = 6.0 - 7.0
Tolerates drought

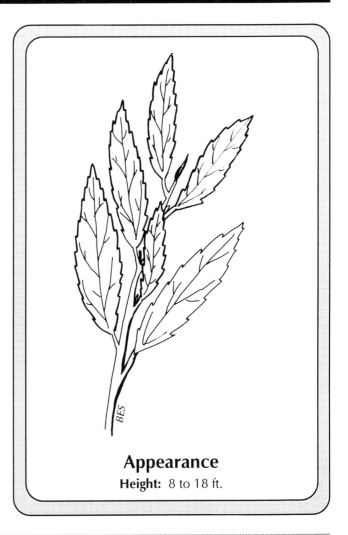

Appearance
Height: 8 to 18 ft.

Wildlife Benefits *(Salix spp.)*
Potential Benefits and Species Served

Food (fruit, buds, flowers): beaver, deer, squirrel, hare, rabbit, moose, porcupine, muskrat, other small game, mallard, northern shoveler, wood duck, green-winged teal, wild turkey, ruffed grouse, bobwhite, ring-necked pheasant, mourning dove, common flicker, yellow-bellied sapsucker; red-bellied, red-headed, hairy, and downy woodpeckers; blue jay, tufted titmouse, white-breasted nuthatch, Carolina wren, brown thrasher, hermit thrush, eastern meadowlark, starling, rusty blackbird, common grackle, cardinal, rose-breasted grosbeak, rufous-sided towhee, pine grosbeak

Cover and Nesting: American crow, northern oriole, scarlet tanager, rose-breasted grosbeak

Hydrology

Indicator status: Facultative wetland

Salinity: fresh water; less than 0.5 ppt

Tidal zone:

Nontidal regime: regularly to permanently inundated or saturated (approximately 26 to 100% of the growing season)

Sambucus canadensis
Elderberry, American elder

Characteristics
Broad-leaved, deciduous shrub

GROWTH
Rate: fast; up to 2 ft. per yr.
Spreads by suckers

PLANTING
Forms available: bare root, container, balled and burlapped

HABITAT
Community: fresh tidal marshes
nontidal marshes
swamps
wet meadows
moist woods
old fields

Distribution: Nova Scotia to Manitoba and South Dakota, south to Florida and Texas

Shade: tolerates full shade; flowers best in partial shade and full sun

NOTES
pH preference = 6.0 - 8.0
Tolerates drought
Susceptible to wind or ice damage (weak wooded)
Grows well on disturbed sites
Plants bear fruit when four years old

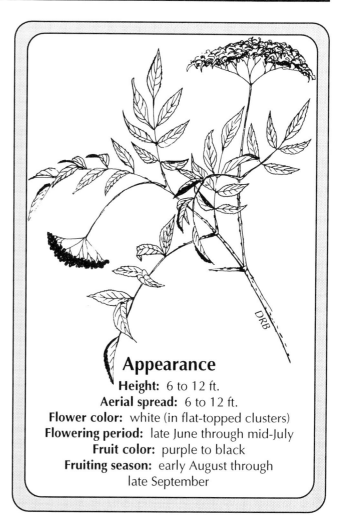

Appearance
Height: 6 to 12 ft.
Aerial spread: 6 to 12 ft.
Flower color: white (in flat-topped clusters)
Flowering period: late June through mid-July
Fruit color: purple to black
Fruiting season: early August through late September

Wildlife Benefits
Potential Benefits and Species Served

Food (fruit): veery*, mourning dove, yellow-bellied sapsucker, eastern kingbird, great-crested flycatcher, American robin, starling, blue jay

Food (fruit) and/or Cover: red-bellied* and red-headed woodpeckers; wood, hermit, Swainson's, and gray-cheeked thrushes; white-throated, chipping, and song sparrows; eastern bluebird*, cedar waxwing*, rose-breasted grosbeak*, rufous-sided towhee*, wild turkey, ring-necked pheasant, common flicker; brown thrasher, yellow-breasted chat, common grackle, cardinal, indigo bunting

Food, Cover, and Nesting: alder flycatcher, mockingbird, gray catbird

Food (twigs, leaves): hoofed browsers

* Preferred food

Environmental Concern Inc.

Hydrology

Indicator status: Facultative wetland –

Salinity: resistant; tolerates infrequent flooding by water containing some salt

Tidal zone: above spring tide to upland

Nontidal regime: irregularly to seasonally inundated or saturated (up to approximately 25% of the growing season)

Vaccinium corymbosom
Highbush blueberry

Characteristics
Broad-leaved, deciduous shrub

GROWTH
Rate: slow; less than 1 ft. per yr.
Spreads by suckers

PLANTING
Forms available: bare root, containter

HABITAT
Community: forested wetlands
 shrub swamps
 bogs
 upland woods (rare)

Distribution: Nova Scotia to southern Quebec, west to Wisconsin, south to Florida and Texas

Shade: tolerates full shade

NOTES
Fairly insenstive to wind or ice damage
Demands acid soil; pH = 3.5 - 6.0 (will tolerate 6.5)

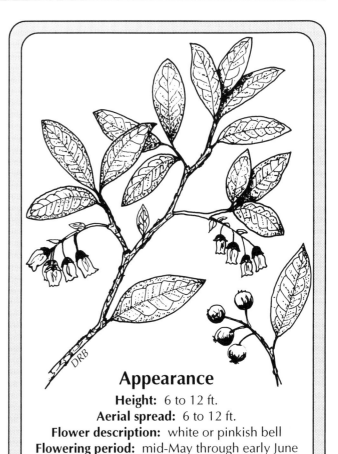

Appearance
Height: 6 to 12 ft.
Aerial spread: 6 to 12 ft.
Flower description: white or pinkish bell
Flowering period: mid-May through early June
Fruit color: bluish to black
Fruiting period: early July through late August

Wildlife Benefits
Potential Benefits and Species Served

Highly valuable fruit

Food (fruit): blue jay, black-capped chickadee, tufted titmouse, brown thrasher, eastern bluebird, orchard oriole, pine grosbeak, scarlet tanager, black bear

Food (fruit), Cover, and/or Nesting: ruffed grouse, ring-necked pheasant, mourning dove, eastern kingbird, gray catbird, American robin, hermit thrush, rufous-sided towhee

Food (plant parts): red fox, skunk, deer, chipmunk, mice

Hydrology

Indicator status: Facultative wetland –

Salinity: resistant; tolerates infrequent flooding by water containing some salt

Tidal zone:

Nontidal regime: seasonally inundated or saturated (approximately 13 to 25% of the growing season)

Viburnum dentatum
Southern arrowwood

Characteristics
Broad-leaved, deciduous shrub

GROWTH
Rate: medium; 1 to 2 ft. per yr.
Spreads by suckers

PLANTING
Forms available: bare root, container, balled and
burlapped

HABITAT
Community: fresh tidal marshes;
nontidal marshes;
shrub swamps;
forested wetlands;
moist woods

Distribution: southeastern Massachusetts, south to
Florida and Texas, west to Pennsylvania, West
Virginia, and Tennessee

Shade: tolerates partial shade

NOTES
Fairly insensitive to wind or ice damage
pH preference = 5.1 - 7.0
Tolerates drought

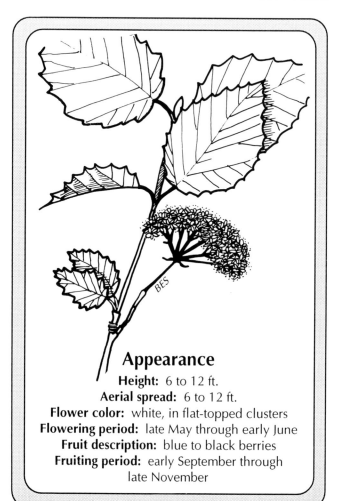

Appearance
Height: 6 to 12 ft.
Aerial spread: 6 to 12 ft.
Flower color: white, in flat-topped clusters
Flowering period: late May through early June
Fruit description: blue to black berries
Fruiting period: early September through
late November

Wildlife Benefits
Potential Benefits and Species Served

Food (fruit): common flicker, eastern phoebe, brown
thrasher, American robin, eastern bluebird, white-
and red-eyed vireos, rose-breasted grosbeak, pileated woodpecker, small mammals

Food (fruit) and Cover and/or Nesting: ruffed grouse,
brown thrasher, gray catbird

Fruit available all winter

Hydrology

Indicator status: Facultative

Salinity: resistant; tolerates infrequent flooding by
water containing some salt

Tidal zone: above spring tide elevation

Nontidal regime: seasonally inundated or saturated
(approximately 13 to 25% of the growing
season)

Viburnum trilobum (V. opulus)
Highbush cranberry, American cranberry bush

Characteristics
Broad-leaved, deciduous shrub

GROWTH
Rate: medium; 1 to 2 ft. per yr.

PLANTING
Forms available: bare root, balled and burlapped

HABITAT
Community: shrub swamps
forested seasonal wetlands
bogs
moist and upland woods

Distribution: Newfoundland to British Columbia, south to New York, Michigan, South Dakota, and Oregon

Shade: tolerates full shade

NOTES
Fairly insensitive to wind or ice damage
pH preference = 6.0 - 7.5
Tolerates drought

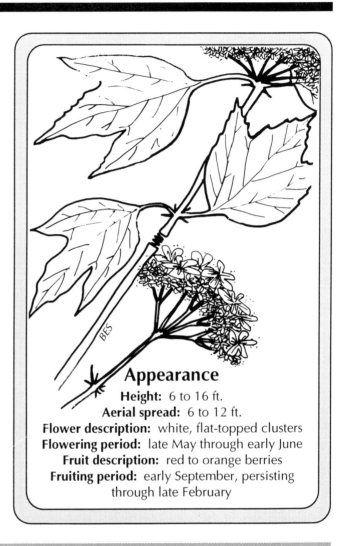

Appearance
Height: 6 to 16 ft.
Aerial spread: 6 to 12 ft.
Flower description: white, flat-topped clusters
Flowering period: late May through early June
Fruit description: red to orange berries
Fruiting period: early September, persisting through late February

Wildlife Benefits
Potential Benefits and Species Served

Food (fruit): eastern bluebird, cedar waxwing, cardinal, pileated woodpecker, small mammals in winter

Food (fruit) and Cover: wild turkey, spruce and ruffed grouse, ring-necked pheasant

Preferred by waxwings
Berries persist into winter, provide emergency food

Hydrology

Indicator status: Facultative wetland

Salinity: fresh water; less than 0.5 ppt

Tidal zone:

Nontidal regime: irregularly or seasonally inundated or saturated (approximately 13 to 25% of the growing season)

PLANT SHEETS

Trees

Acer negundo
Box elder, Ash-leaved maple

Characteristics
Broad-leaved, deciduous tree

GROWTH
Rate: fast; 15 to 20 ft. in 5 yrs.

PLANTING
Forms available: container

HABITAT
Community: forested seasonal wetlands
alluvial woods

Distribution: New Hampshire and Vermont to southern Ontario, Montana, and Wyoming, south to Florida and Texas

Shade: requires full sun

NOTES
Susceptible to wind or ice damage (weak wooded)
Susceptible to Anthracnose, powdery mildew, and several canker diseases
Susceptible to boxelder bug, striped maple worm, and many species of borers
pH preference = 6.0 - 8.0 (will tolerate 5.0)
Tolerates drought
Male and female flowers on separate plants

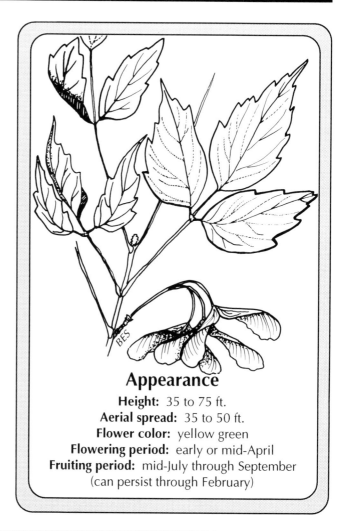

Appearance
Height: 35 to 75 ft.
Aerial spread: 35 to 50 ft.
Flower color: yellow green
Flowering period: early or mid-April
Fruiting period: mid-July through September
(can persist through February)

Wildlife Benefits
Potential Benefits and Species Served

Food (seeds): ring-necked pheasant, evening grosbeak, purple finch, pine grosbeak, waterbirds, songbirds, squirrels, mice

Cover: yellow warbler, evening grosbeak

Nesting: yellow warbler, purple finch, songbirds

Food (young twigs, leaves): white-tailed deer, other hoofed browsers

Hydrology

Indicator status: Facultative +

Salinity: resistant; tolerates infrequent flooding by water containing some salt

Tidal zone: near mean high water and above to spring tide elevation

Nontidal regime: irregularly, seasonally, or regularly inundated or saturated (tolerates frequent, temporary inundation up to approximately 75% of the growing season)

Acer rubrum
Red maple

Characteristics
Broad-leaved, deciduous tree

GROWTH
Rate: medium to fast; 18 to 25 ft. in 10 yrs.

PLANTING
Forms available: seed, plug, whip, bare root, container, balled and burlapped

HABITAT
Community: fresh tidal marsh or swamp
nontidal marsh or swamp
alluvial woods
moist uplands

Distribution: Quebec to Manitoba, south to southern Florida, Oklahoma, and Texas

Shade: tolerates partial shade

NOTES
Small transplants do not tolerate standing water
Susceptible to wind or ice damage (weak wooded)
Susceptible to rot-causing fungi, canker injuries, and Verticillium wilt
Susceptible to leaf hoppers, many borers, and scale
pH preference = 4.5 - 7.0
Tolerates drought
Male and female flowers usually on separate plants

Appearance
Height: 75 to 100 ft.
Aerial spread: 50 to 75 ft.
Colors: red flowers and buds
Flowering period: late March, early April
Fruiting period: late April to mid June

Wildlife Benefits
Potential Benefits and Species Served

Food (seed, sap, or buds): bobwhite, yellow-bellied sapsucker, cardinal, evening and pine grosbeaks, waterbirds, squirrels, chipmunk

Cover and Nesting: American robin, prairie warbler, American goldfinch

Food (twigs, foliage): hoofed browsers

Hydrology

Indicator status: Facultative to Facultative wetland +

Salinity: fresh water; less than 0.5 ppt

Tidal zone: above spring tide elevation

Nontidal regime: irregularly to seasonally inundated or saturated (up to approximately 25% of the growing season)

Acer saccharinum
Silver maple, White maple, Soft maple, River maple

Characteristics
Broad-leaved, deciduous tree

GROWTH
Rate: fast; 25 to 35 ft. in 10 yrs.

PLANTING
Forms available: plug, container, balled and burlapped

HABITAT
Community: forested seasonal wetlands
alluvial woods
river banks

Distribution: New Brunswick to Ontario and Minnesota, South Dakota, south to Florida, Oklahoma, Louisiana

Shade: tolerates partial shade

NOTES
Susceptible to wind or ice damage (weak wooded)
Susceptible to Anthracnose, Verticillium wilt, and Nectria canker
Susceptible to ocellate leaf gall, cottony maple scale, borers, and other scale
pH preference = 5.5 - 7.0
Tolerates drought
Male and female flowers mostly on separate plants

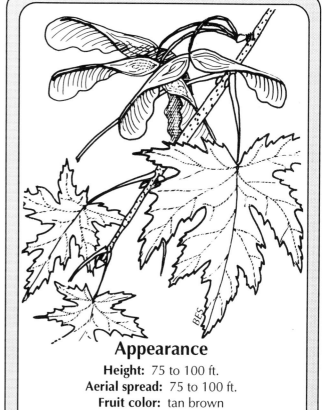

Appearance
Height: 75 to 100 ft.
Aerial spread: 75 to 100 ft.
Fruit color: tan brown
Flower color: red (female) or yellow (male)
Flowering period: March
Fruiting period: April to May

Wildlife Benefits
Potential Benefits and Species Served

Food (seeds or buds): bobwhite, cardinal, evening and pine grosbeaks

Cover and Nesting: northern oriole, American goldfinch

Food (twigs, foliage): hoofed browsers

Hydrology

Indicator status: Facultative wetland

Salinity: resistant; tolerates infrequent flooding by water containing some salt

Tidal zone: above spring tide elevation

Nontidal regime: irregularly to seasonally inundated or saturated (up to approximately 25% of the growing season)

Amelanchier canadensis
Serviceberry, Shadbush, Oblong-leaf Juneberry, Shadblow serviceberry

Characteristics
Broad-leaved, deciduous tree

GROWTH
Rate: medium; approximately 2.5 ft. per yr.

PLANTING
Forms available: container, balled and burlapped

HABITAT
Community: shrub swamps
forested wetlands

Distribution: Newfoundland to Mississippi on Coastal Plain

Shade: tolerates full shade

NOTES
Tolerates drought
pH preference = 5.0 - 6.5
Relatively insensitive to disease, insect, and wind or ice damage

DRB

Appearance
Height: 35 to 50 ft.
Aerial spread: 35 to 50 ft.
Flower color: white
Flowering period: mid- through late April
Fruit color: dark purple to black
Fruiting period: mid-June through mid-July

Wildlife Benefits
Potential Benefits and Species Served

Food (fruit): ruffed grouse; hairy, downy, and red-headed woodpeckers; tufted titmouse, red-winged blackbird, eastern bluebird, cedar waxwing, mourning dove, common flicker, eastern phoebe, blue jay, brown thrasher, red-eyed vireo, American redstart, northern oriole, scarlet tanager, cardinal, rose-breasted grosbeak, northern junco, song sparrow

Cover and Nesting: eastern kingbird, American robin; wood, hermit, and Swainson's thrushes

Hydrology

Indicator status: Facultative

Salinity: resistant; tolerates infrequent flooding by water containing some salt

Tidal zone:

Nontidal regime: irregularly to seasonally inundated or saturated (up to approximately 25% of the growing season)

Betula nigra
River birch

Characteristics
Broad-leaved, deciduous tree

GROWTH
Rate: fast; 30 to 40 ft. in 10 yrs.

PLANTING
Forms available: seed, plug, container, balled and burlapped

HABITAT
Community: forested seasonal wetlands
floodplain forests
streambanks

Distribution: New Hampshire to Minnesota, south to Florida and Texas

Shade: requires full sun

NOTES
Roots readily from cuttings
Susceptible to wind or ice damage (weak wooded)
Tolerates drought
Used for streambank stabilization
If seed source available, colonizes adjacent sites readily

Appearance
Height: 50 to 75 ft.
Aerial spread: 35 to 50 ft.
Flower color: light green to yellow green
Flowering period: late April through early May
Fruiting period: June to early August

Wildlife Benefits
Potential Benefits and Species Served

Food (seeds): sharp-tailed, ruffed, and spruce grouse, redpoll, pine siskin, wild turkey

Food (twigs, foliage): moose, white-tailed deer, beaver, hare, porcupine

Hydrology

Indicator status: Facultative wetland

Salinity: fresh water; less than 0.5 ppt

Tidal zone:

Nontidal regime: irregularly to seasonally inundated or saturated (up to approximately 25% of the growing season)

Betula populifolia
Gray birch, White birch, Fire birch, Oldfield birch

Characteristics
Broad-leaved, deciduous tree

GROWTH
Rate: fast; 2 to 2.5 ft. per yr. in the first 10 yrs.
Spreads by suckers

PLANTING
Forms available: seed

HABITAT
Community: forested seasonal wetlands

Distribution: Quebec west to southwestern Ontario
south to Nova Scotia, New England, Delaware,
Pennsylvania, upland Virginia, northern Ohio,
northern Indiana

Shade: requires full sun

NOTES
Pioneer species, does well in poor, almost sterile soils;
does well in disturbed areas
Seeds well and forms thickets from suckers
Tolerates drought

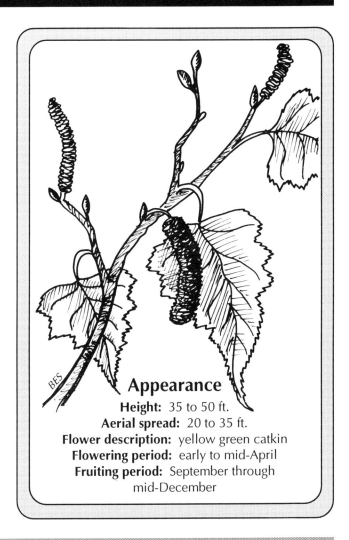

Appearance
Height: 35 to 50 ft.
Aerial spread: 20 to 35 ft.
Flower description: yellow green catkin
Flowering period: early to mid-April
Fruiting period: September through
mid-December

Wildlife Benefits
Potential Benefits and Species Served

Food (seed): green-winged teal, wood duck, bufflehead,
great blue heron, wild turkey, ring-necked pheasant,
blue jay, black-capped chickadee, northern junco,
tufted titmouse, common redpoll, pine siskin,
American goldfinch

Food (flower clusters, buds): grouse, squirrel

Cover and Nesting: black-capped chickadee

Grazing: hoofed browsers

Hydrology

Indicator status: Facultative

Salinity: resistant; tolerates infrequent flooding by
water containing some salt

Tidal zone:

Nontidal regime: irregularly, seasonally, or regularly
inundated or saturated (tolerates frequent temporary inundation up to approximately 75% of the
growing season)

Celtis occidentalis
Hackberry, Sugarberry

Characteristics
Broad-leaved, deciduous tree

GROWTH
Rate: medium; 22 in. to 2.5 ft. per yr.

PLANTING
Forms available: bare root plant, balled and burlapped

HABITAT
Community: forested seasonal wetlands
river banks

Distribution: Quebec to Manitoba, south to Florida, Tennessee, Arkansas, and Oklahoma (varieties occur accross this range)

Shade: tolerates full shade

NOTES
Seedlings cannot tolerate submergence
Good shrub for buffer area
pH preference = 6.6 - 8.0
Susceptible to Witches' broom, Powdery mildew, leaf spots, hackberry nipple gall, Morning cloak butterfly, and scales
Tolerates drought
Adapts to a variety of soils; grows in limestone soils

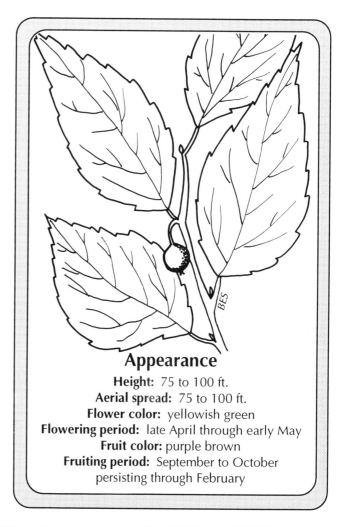

Appearance
Height: 75 to 100 ft.
Aerial spread: 75 to 100 ft.
Flower color: yellowish green
Flowering period: late April through early May
Fruit color: purple brown
Fruiting period: September to October persisting through February

Wildlife Benefits
Potential Benefits and Species Served

Food (fruit): upland gamebirds (e.g., bobwhite, pheasant, wild turkey, grouse), songbirds (e.g., mockingbird, American robin), terrestrial furbearers, small mammals (e.g., squirrels, raccoon)

Food (twigs, foliage): deer

Hydrology

Indicator status: Facultative upland

Salinity: resistant; tolerates infrequent flooding by water containing some salt

Tidal zone:

Nontidal regime: irregularly to seasonally inundated (seedlings cannot tolerate submergence) or saturated (up to approximately 25% of the growing season)

Chamaecyparis thyoides
Atlantic white cedar, False cypress, Swamp cedar, Southern white cedar

Characteristics
Needle-leaved, evergreen tree

GROWTH
Rate: medium; 25 ft. in 20 yrs.

PLANTING
Forms available: container

HABITAT
Community: forested wetlands
            shrub bogs
            edges of streams

Distribution: central Maine, south to northern Florida
     and Mississippi

Shade: prefers full sun

NOTES
Cannot compete with hardwood species
Usually grow on hummocks
pH preference = 3.0 - 5.0
For more information refer to Laderman 1989

Appearance
Height: 40 to 50 ft.
Aerial spread: 10 to 20 ft.
Cone description: small, bluish, globe-shaped
Fruiting period: April into fall

Wildlife Benefits
Potential Benefits and Species Served

Food and Winter browse: white-tailed deer, pine siskin

Food (seedlings): cottontail rabbit, meadow mouse

Food: Hessel's hairstreak butterfly

Community: bear, beaver, otter, deer; parula, prairie, prothonotory, hooded, and worm-eating warblers; Cooper's and red-shouldered hawks, barred owl, ovenbird, yellowthroat, others

Hydrology

Indicator status: Obligate wetland

Salinity: fresh water; less than 0.5 ppt

Tidal zone: rarely found in tidal areas and only those which are infrequently subject to tidal flow

Nontidal regime: irregularly to semipermanently inundated or saturated (up to nearly 100% of the growing season); communities usually have fluctuating water (table) depth

Fraxinus nigra
Black ash

Characteristics
Broad-leaved, deciduous tree

GROWTH
Rate: fast; 2 to 3 ft. per yr.

PLANTING
Forms available: seed, bare root

HABITAT
Community: forested wetlands

Distribution: southern Quebec and southern Ontario, south to Delaware, Virginia, West Virginia, Ohio, Indiana, Illinois, Iowa, west to Minnesota and South Dakota

Shade: requires full sun

NOTES
pH preference = 4.6 to 6.5
Tolerates drought
Male and female flowers on separate plants
Susceptible to leaf spot, Anthracnose, rust, canker, oystershell scale, and ash borer
Susceptible to wind or ice damage (brittle twigs)

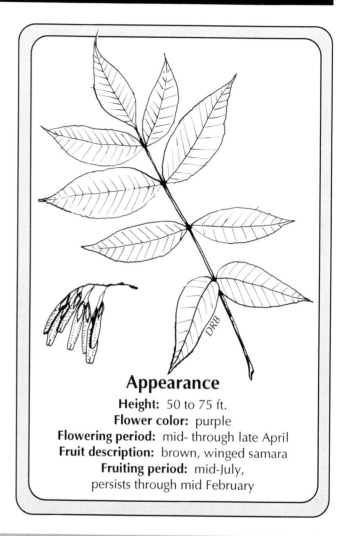

Appearance
Height: 50 to 75 ft.
Flower color: purple
Flowering period: mid- through late April
Fruit description: brown, winged samara
Fruiting period: mid-July, persists through mid February

Wildlife Benefits (*Fraxinus spp.*)
Potential Benefits and Species Served

Food (seeds): wood duck, wild turkey, bobwhite, red-winged blackbird, rusty blackbird, cardinal, purple finch, pine grosbeak

Food (sap): yellow-bellied sapsucker

Food (leaves, bark): cottontail rabbit

Cover, Nesting: mourning dove, evening grosbeak

Browsing: white-tailed deer

Hydrology

Indicator status: Facultative wetland

Salinity: resistant; tolerates infrequent flooding by water containing some salt

Tidal zone: above mean high water

Nontidal regime: irregularly to seasonally inundated or saturated (up to approximately 25% of the growing season)

Fraxinus pennsylvanica
Green ash

Characteristics
Broad-leaved, deciduous tree

GROWTH
Rate: fast; 2.5 to 3 ft. per yr.

PLANTING
Forms available: bare root, container, balled and burlapped

HABITAT
Community: tidal freshwater forested wetlands
nontidal forested wetlands

Distribution: Maine, Ontario, and Saskatchewan, south to Florida and Texas

Shade: tolerates partial shade

NOTES
Susceptible to wind or ice damage (brittle twigs)
Fairly insensitive to disease
Some varieties susceptible to ash borer, oystershell scale, brown headed ash sawfly, lilac leaf minor, and lilac borer
Competes well in wide variety of conditions
pH preference = 6.1 - 7.5
Male and female flowers on separate plants
Tolerates drought

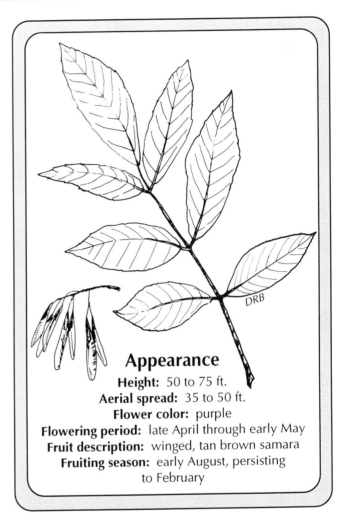

Appearance
Height: 50 to 75 ft.
Aerial spread: 35 to 50 ft.
Flower color: purple
Flowering period: late April through early May
Fruit description: winged, tan brown samara
Fruiting season: early August, persisting to February

Wildlife Benefits (*Fraxinus spp.*)
Potential Benefits and Species Served

Food (seeds): wood duck, bobwhite, red-winged blackbird, cardinal, purple finch, wild turkey, rusty blackbird, evening and pine grosbeaks; squirrels

Food (sap): yellow-bellied sapsucker

Cover and Nesting: mourning dove, evening grosbeak

Browsing: white-tailed deer, moose

Hydrology

Indicator status: Facultative wetland

Salinity: resistant; tolerates infrequent flooding by water containing some salt

Tidal zone: above mean high water to upland

Nontidal regime: irregularly, seasonally, or regularly inundated or saturated (tolerates frequent, temporary flooding up to approximately 75% of the growing season)

Environmental Concern Inc.

Liquidambar styraciflua
American sweetgum

Characteristics
Broad-leaved, deciduous tree

GROWTH
Rate: slow to medium; 1 to 2 ft. per yr.
Spreads by suckers

PLANTING
Forms available: seed, plug, bare root seedling, container, balled and burlapped

HABITAT
Community: forested seasonal wetlands
moist upland woods
clearings

Distribution: southern Connecticut to southern Illinois and Oklahoma, south to Florida and Mexico

Shade: requires full sun

NOTES
Fairly insensitive to disease, insect, and wind or ice
damage
On high pH soils, susceptible to iron chlorosis
pH preference = 6.0 - 7.0
Tolerates drought
Does best on rich, moist, alluvial soils

Appearance
Height: 75 to 100 ft.
Aerial spread: 50 to 75 ft.
Flower color: yellow green
Flowering period: late April through early May
Fruit description: horny, woody ball
Fruiting period: July, persisting through January

Wildlife Benefits
Potential Benefits and Species Served

Food (seeds): mallard, wild turkey, bobwhite, rock dove, mourning dove, yellow-bellied sapsucker, black-capped and Carolina chickadees, Carolina wren, starling, red-winged blackbird, cardinal, evening grosbeak, purple finch, common redpoll, pine siskin, American goldfinch, rufous-sided towhee, northern junco, white-crowned and white-throated sparrows, gray squirrel

Hydrology

Indicator status: Facultative

Salinity: resistant; tolerates infrequent flooding by water containing some salt

Tidal zone: above mean high water to upland

Nontidal regime: irregularly, seasonally, or regularly inundated or saturated (up to approximately 75% of the growing season)

Nyssa sylvatica
Black gum, Black tupelo, Sour gum

Characteristics
Broad-leaved, deciduous tree

GROWTH
Rate: slow; 4 to 5 in. per yr.
Spreads by suckers

PLANTING
Forms available: seed, bare root, container, balled and
burlapped

HABITAT
Community: forested seasonal wetlands;
moist upland woods;
dry woods

Distribution: Maine to southern Ontario, south to
Florida and Texas

Shade: tolerates partial shade

NOTES
pH preference = 6.0 - 7.0
Fairly insensitive to disease, insect, and wind or ice
damage
Male and female flowers on separate plants
Tolerates drought

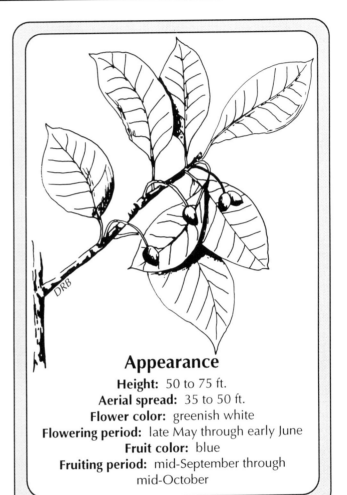

Appearance
Height: 50 to 75 ft.
Aerial spread: 35 to 50 ft.
Flower color: greenish white
Flowering period: late May through early June
Fruit color: blue
Fruiting period: mid-September through
mid-October

Wildlife Benefits
Potential Benefits and Species Served

Food (fruit): wood duck, common flicker, cedar waxwing, summer tanager, red-headed and pileated
woodpeckers, wood thrush, American robin, aquatic
and terrestrial furbearers (e.g., fox, black bear)

Hollow trunks: raccoon, owls

Food (twigs, foliage): deer, beaver

Hydrology

Indicator status: Facultative

Salinity: resistant; tolerates infrequent flooding by
water containing some salt

Tidal zone: above mean high water (in <u>fresh</u> water)
to upland

Nontidal regime: irregularly to seasonally inundated
or saturated (up to approximately 25% of the
growing season)

Environmental Concern Inc.

Pinus rigida
Pitch pine

Characteristics
Needle-leaved, evergreen tree

GROWTH
Rate: fast; 2 to 3 ft. per yr. (slow during first 5 yrs., then increases)

PLANTING
Forms available: container

HABITAT
Community: pine barrens

Distribution: southeastern Maine to eastern Ontario, western New York, northwestern Pennsylvania, and eastern Ohio, south to Virginia, mountains of Georgia, eastern Tennessee, and Kentucky

Shade: requires full sun

NOTES
Found mostly in sandy soils; does well in poor soils

Susceptible to gall rusts, needle cast, needle blight, and heart rot diseases

Susceptible to tip moth, pitch pine looper, sawflies, pine webworm, pine needle miner

Snow and ice cause leader and limb damage

pH preference = 4.6 – 6.5

Tolerates drought

Fire assists in opening cones

Appearance
Height: 50 to 75 ft.
Aerial spread: 50 to 75 ft.
Flower description: red purple cone
Flowering period: May
Fruit description: tan brown cone
Fruiting period: persist for many seasons

Wildlife Benefits
Potential Benefits and Species Served

Very high wildlife value

Food (seeds): pine warbler, pine grosbeak, black-capped chickadee, other songbirds, upland birds, and small mammals

Food (sprouts, seedlings): white-tailed deer, rabbits

Produces cones at an early age (12 yr. old trees produce quantities of seeds)

Hydrology

Indicator status: Facultative upland

Salinity: resistant; tolerates infrequent flooding by water containing some salt

Tidal zone:

Nontidal regime: irregularly to seasonally inundated or saturated (up to approximately 25% of the growing season)

Pinus taeda
Loblolly pine

Characteristics
Needle-leaved, evergreen tree

GROWTH
Rate: fast; approximately 2 ft. or more per yr.

PLANTING
Forms available: seed, plug, bare root plant, container, balled and burlapped

HABITAT
Community: forested seasonal wetland
moist sandy soil
abandoned fields and pine plantations

Distribution: southern New Jersey to Florida and Texas, west to Tennessee and Oklahoma

Shade:

NOTES
Susceptible to pine beetle and fusiform rust diseases
Good pioneer species; aggressive; adaptable to extremes of soil
Tolerates drought
pH preference = 5.0 - 6.5

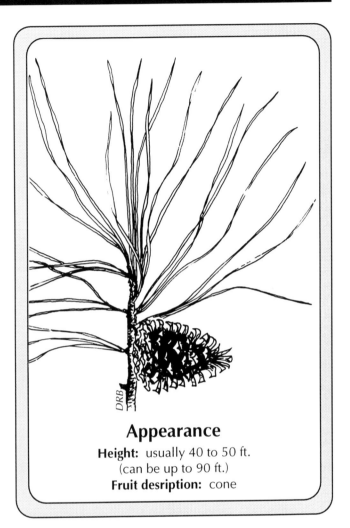

Appearance
Height: usually 40 to 50 ft.
(can be up to 90 ft.)
Fruit desription: cone

Wildlife Benefits
Potential Benefits and Species Served

Food (seeds): squirrels, chipmunks, mice, other rodents, bobwhite, wild turkey

May produce seed at 10 yrs. although 30 to 40 yrs. is average
Important because of abundance of seed produced

Hydrology

Indicator status: Facultative –

Salinity: resistant; tolerates infrequent flooding by water containing some salt

Tidal zone: above spring tide to upland

Nontidal regime: irregularly, seasonally, or regularly inundated or saturated (up to approximately 50% of the growing season with periods of dry-down)

Platanus occidentalis
Sycamore, Buttonwood, Planetree

Characteristics
Broad-leaved, deciduous tree

GROWTH
Rate: very fast; up to 70 ft. in 20 yr. period

PLANTING
Forms available: seed, bare root plant, plug, container, balled and burlapped

HABITAT
Community: forested seasonal wetlands
lake and swamp edges
moist alluvial woods
dry slopes

Distribution: southern Maine to Minnesota, south to Florida and Texas

Shade: tolerates partial shade

NOTES
Susceptible to Anthracnose and leaf spot diseases
Fairly insensitive to insect and wind or ice damage
pH preference = 6.0 – 8.0
Tolerates drought

Appearance
Height: 75 to 100 ft.
Aerial spread: 75 to 100 ft.
Flower color: yellow green
Flowering period: late May through early June
Fruit description: tan brown, globular
Fruiting period: early August, persisting to late December

Wildlife Benefits
Potential Benefits and Species Served

Low food value

Food (seeds): songbirds, terrestrial furbearers, aquatic furbearers

Food (twigs, buds): deer, muskrat

Dens: wood duck, opossum, raccoon

Hydrology

Indicator status: Facultative wetland –

Salinity: fresh water; less than 0.5 ppt

Tidal zone:

Nontidal regime: irregularly to seasonally inundated or saturated (up to approximately 25% of the growing season)

Populus deltoides
Eastern cottonwood

Characteristics
Broad-leaved, deciduous tree

GROWTH
Rate: fast; 4 to 5 ft. per yr. (120 ft. in 35 yr. period is common on wet sites)

PLANTING
Forms available: bare root plant; container

HABITAT
Community: forested seasonal wetlands

Distribution: southwestern Quebec to Manitoba, south to northern Florida and Texas

Shade: requires full sun

NOTES
Susceptible to poplar canker, Cytospora canker, Fusarium canker, leaf blister, branch gall, dieback, bronze birch borer, poplar borer, poplar tent maker
Weak wooded
pH preference = 6.6 – 7.5
Male and female flowers on separate plants
Trees easily clog sewers with roots
Grows well from cuttings

Appearance
Height: 75 to 100 ft.
Aerial spread: 75 to 100 ft.
Flower description: bright red catkins
Flowering period: mid- through late April
Fruit description: yellow green capsules
Fruiting period: late May through mid-June

Wildlife Benefits
Potential Benefits and Species Served

Food (buds, catkins): ruffed grouse, evening grosbeak, purple finch, upland gamebirds, songbirds, waterfowl

Food (sap): yellow-bellied sapsucker

Food (bark, foliage): aquatic furbearers, terrestrial furbearers, small mammals, hoofed browsers

Hydrology

Indicator status: Facultative

Salinity: resistant; tolerates infrequent flooding by water containing some salt

Tidal zone:

Nontidal regime: seasonally inundated or saturated (approximately 13 to 25% of the growing season)

Environmental Concern Inc.

Quercus bicolor
Swamp white oak

Characteristics
Broad-leaved, deciduous tree

GROWTH
Rate: fast; 1.5 to 2 ft. per yr. (slows as matures)

PLANTING
Forms available: bare root, container

HABITAT
Community: forested seasonal wetlands

Distribution: Maine and Quebec to Minnesota, south to Virginia and Missouri, upland Georgia, Kentucky, Arkansas, and Oklahoma

Shade: tolerates partial shade

NOTES
pH preference = 5.0 - 7.5
Susceptible to iron chlorosis and gypsy moths
Fairly insensitive to disease, insect, and wind or ice damage
Tolerates drought

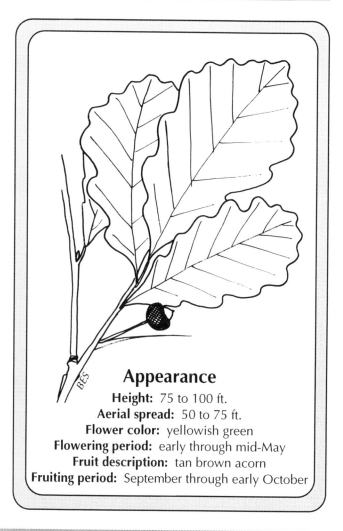

Appearance
Height: 75 to 100 ft.
Aerial spread: 50 to 75 ft.
Flower color: yellowish green
Flowering period: early through mid-May
Fruit description: tan brown acorn
Fruiting period: September through early October

Wildlife Benefits
Potential Benefits and Species Served

Food (acorns, buds): waterfowl (esp. wood duck), marshbirds, shorebirds, upland gamebirds, songbirds (esp. common grackle, blue jay, brown thrasher, red-bellied and red-headed woodpeckers), raccoon, squirrel, chipmunk, white-footed mouse

Food (twigs, foliage, acorns): deer

Dens

Begins producing acorns at 25 to 30 yrs.

Hydrology

Indicator status: Facultative wetland +

Salinity: resistant; tolerates infrequent flooding by water containing some salt

Tidal zone:

Nontidal regime: irregularly to seasonally inundated or saturated (up to approximately 25% of the growing season)

Quercus nigra
Water oak, Possum oak

Characteristics
Broad-leaved, deciduous tree

GROWTH
Rate: fast (in well-drained soils); approximately 2 ft. or more per yr.

PLANTING
Forms available: bare root plant, plug, container, balled and burlapped

HABITAT
Community: forested seasonal wetlands
stream borders
moist alluvial and upland woods

Distribution: Delaware to southeastern Missouri and Ohio, south to Florida and Texas (chiefly on Coastal Plain)

Shade:

NOTES
pH preference = 5.0 - 6.0
Susceptible to gypsy moths

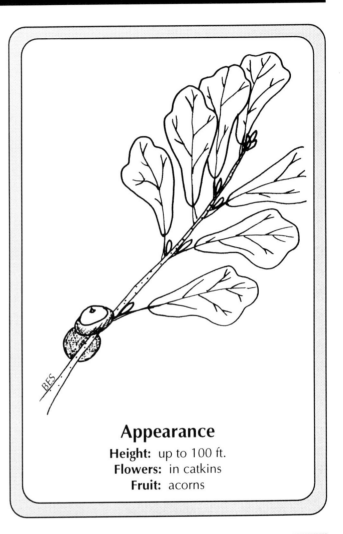

Appearance
Height: up to 100 ft.
Flowers: in catkins
Fruit: acorns

Wildlife Benefits
Potential Benefits and Species Served

Cover, Nesting

Food (acorns): mammals (gray squirrel), wood duck

Begins producing acorns at 20 yrs.

Hydrology

Indicator status: Facultative

Salinity: fresh water; less than 0.5 ppt

Tidal zone: above spring tide elevation

Nontidal regime: seasonally inundated or saturated (approximately 13 to 25% of the growing season)

Environmental Concern Inc.

Quercus palustris
Pin oak, Spanish oak

Characteristics
Broad-leaved, deciduous tree

GROWTH
Rate: fast; 30 ft. in 12 to 15 yrs.

PLANTING
Forms available: bare root, plug, container, balled and burlapped

HABITAT
Community: forested seasonal wetlands
moist alluvial woods

Distribution: Vermont and southern Ontario, south to North Carolina and Oklahoma

Shade: requires full sun

NOTES
Seedlings intolerant to standing water
pH preference = 5.0 - 6.5
Susceptible to iron chlorosis and gypsy moths
Fairly insensitive to disease, insect, and wind or ice damage
Tolerates drought

Appearance
Height: 50 to 75 ft.
Aerial spreading: 50 to 75 ft.
Flower color: yellow green
Flowering period: early through mid-May
Fruit description: red brown acorn
Fruiting period: September through early October

Wildlife Benefits
Potential Benefits and Species Served

Food: wood duck, mallard, wild turkey, ruffed grouse, bobwhite, blue jay, brown thrasher, rufous-sided towhee, woodpeckers, deer, fox, opossum, raccoon

Cover and Nesting: scarlet tanager, rose-breasted grosbeak

Begins producing acorns at 15 to 25 yrs.

Hydrology

Indicator status: Facultative wetland

Salinity: resistant; tolerates infrequent flooding by water containing some salt

Tidal zone:

Nontidal regime: irregularly to seasonally inundated or saturated (up to approximately 25% of the growing season)

Quercus phellos
Willow oak

Characteristics
Broad-leaved, deciduous tree

GROWTH
Rate: fast; 2 ft. per yr.

PLANTING
Forms available: bare root, plug, container, balled and burlapped

HABITAT
Community: forested seasonal wetlands
moist alluvial woods

Distribution: southern New York to southern Illinois, south to Florida and Texas

Shade: tolerates partial shade

NOTES
Tolerates drought
pH preference = 5.0 - 6.0
Susceptible to gypsy moths

Appearance
Height: 40 to 60 ft.
Aerial spread: 30 to 40 ft.
Fruit description: brown acorn
Fruiting period: April to May

Wildlife Benefits
Potential Benefits and Species Served

Food, Cover, and Nesting: wood duck, mallard, bob-white, wild turkey, common grackle, ruffed grouse, green-winged teal, red-bellied woodpecker, fox, opossum, raccoon, squirrel, deer

Begins producing acorns at 20 yrs.

Hydrology

Indicator status: Facultative +

Salinity: fresh water; less than 0.5 ppt

Tidal zone:

Nontidal regime: irregularly to seasonally inundated or saturated (up to approximately 25% of the growing season)

Salix nigra
Black willow

Characteristics
Broad-leaved, deciduous tree

GROWTH
Rate: very fast; 3 to 6 ft. per yr.
Spreads by suckers

PLANTING
Forms available: bare root, container

HABITAT
Community: fresh tidal marshes
fresh tidal swamps
forested wetlands
floodplains
wet meadows

Distribution: southern Canada to central Minnesota, south to Florida and Texas

Shade: requires full sun

NOTES
Used for streambank stabilization
Susceptible to fungus scab and black canker
Susceptible to wind and ice damage (weak wooded)
pH preference = 6.0 – 8.0
Cuttings root readily

Appearance
Height: 35 to 50 ft.
Aerial spread: 20 to 35 ft.
Flower color: yellow green
Flowering period: mid-March through early April
Fruit description: green yellow strobile
Fruiting period: late April until mid-May

Wildlife Benefits (*Salix spp.*)
Potential Benefits and Species Served

Food (fruit, buds, flowers): beaver, deer, squirrel, hare, rabbit, moose, porcupine, muskrat, other small game, mallard, northern shoveler, wood duck, green-winged teal, wild turkey, ruffed grouse*, bobwhite, ring-necked pheasant, mourning dove; red-bellied, red-headed, hairy, and downy woodpeckers; flicker, yellow-bellied sapsucker, blue jay, tufted titmouse, white-breasted nuthatch, Carolina wren, brown thrasher, hermit thrush, starling, meadowlark, rusty blackbird, common grackle, Cardinal, rose-breasted grosbeak, rufous-sided towhee, pine grosbeak*

Cover and Nesting: American crow, northern oriole, scarlet tanager, rose-breasted grosbeak

* *Salix nigra* is the preferred food source of these species

Hydrology

Indicator status: Facultative wetland +

Salinity: fresh water; less than 0.5 ppt

Tidal zone: near mean high water and above to spring tide elevation

Nontidal regime: irregularly, seasonally, or regularly inundated or saturated (up to approximately 75% of the growing season with intermittent periods of dry-down)

Taxodium distichum
Bald cypress

Characteristics
Needle-leaved, deciduous tree

GROWTH
Rate: medium; 1 to 2 ft. per yr. for the first 50 yrs.

PLANTING
Forms available: seed, bare root plant, plug, container

HABITAT
Community: fresh tidal swamps
forested wetlands
fiver banks
open water (sometimes)

Distribution: southern New Jersey, south to Florida and Texas, Mississippi Valley north to southern Illinois and Indiana

Shade: tolerates partial shade; seedlings prefer full sun

NOTES
Susceptible to iron chlorosis on neutral or alkaline soils
Prefers acid soil; pH = 5.0 - 6.5
Fairly insensitive to wind and ice damage
Seed germination requires draw-down (for oxygen supply)
Seedlings cannot tolerate long periods of inundation during the growing season
For more information refer to Brandt and Ewel 1989

Appearance
Height: 75 to 100 ft.
Aerial spread: 20 to 35 ft.
Flower description: deep purple, drooping cone
Flowering period: mid-March through early April
Fruit description: purple brown, globular cone
Fruiting period: early October through December

Wildlife Benefits
Potential Benefits and Species Served

Low food value

Perching site or Nesting (hollow trunks): great blue heron, wild turkey, owls, woodpeckers, warblers

Food (seed): sandhill crane

Hydrology

Indicator status: Obligate wetland

Salinity: fresh water; less than 0.5 ppt

Tidal zone: from mid-tide to upland

Nontidal regime: irregularly, seasonally, regularly, or permanently inundated or saturated (up to 100% of the growing season)

Thuja occidentalis
Northern white cedar, Arbor vitae

Characteristics
Needle-leaved, evergreen tree

GROWTH
Rate: medium to fast; 2 ft. per yr. (can be slower in wetland areas)

PLANTING
Forms available: container, balled and burlapped

HABITAT
Community: forested swamps
shrub swamps
bogs
forested seasonal wetlands

Distribution: eastern Quebec to Saskatchewan, south to Nova Scotia, northern and western New England, New York, south along mountains to North Carolina and Tennessee, Ohio, northern Indiana, northeastern Illinois, Wisconsin, Minnesota

Shade: tolerates partial shade

NOTES
Susceptible to wind or ice damage (weak wooded)
pH preference = 6.0 - 8.0

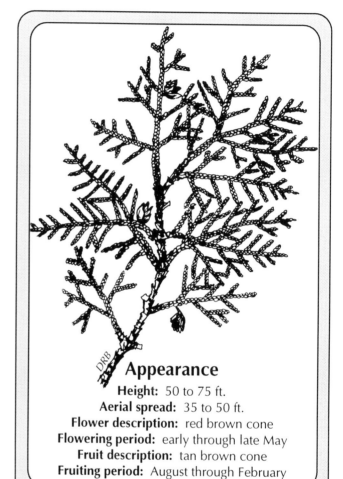

Appearance
Height: 50 to 75 ft.
Aerial spread: 35 to 50 ft.
Flower description: red brown cone
Flowering period: early through late May
Fruit description: tan brown cone
Fruiting period: August through February

Wildlife Benefits
Potential Benefits and Species Served

Low value for wildlife

Food (buds): red squirrel

Food (browse): snowshoe hare, white-tailed deer, moose, cottontail

Food (seeds): pine siskin

Cover

Hydrology

Indicator status: Facultative wetland

Salinity: fresh water; less than 0.5 ppt

Tidal zone:

Nontidal regime: seasonally or regularly saturated (approximately 13 to 75% of the growing season)

Ulmus americana
American elm, White elm

Characteristics
Broad-leaved, deciduous tree

GROWTH
Rate: medium; 20 ft. in 10 yrs.

PLANTING
Forms available: seed, plug, container, balled and burlapped

HABITAT
Community: forested seasonal wetlands
moist, rich upland woods

Distribution: Newfoundland to Saskatchewan, south to northern Florida, Louisiana, and Texas

Shade: tolerates full shade

NOTES
Susceptible to Dutch Elm disease, cankers, Verticillium wilt
Susceptible to gypsy moth, bark beetles, elm borer, cankerworms, elm cockscomb gall
Fairly insensitive to wind or ice damage
pH preference = 6.0 - 8.0
Tolerates drought

Appearance
Height: 75 to 100 ft.
Aerial spread: 75 to 100 ft.
Flower color: red brown
Flowering period: early through mid-April
Fruit description: tan brown samara
Fruiting period: throughout May

Wildlife Benefits
Potential Benefits and Species Served

Food (seed and/or buds or sap): wood duck, wild turkey, ruffed grouse, bobwhite, ring-necked pheasant, yellow-rumped warbler, house sparrow, cardinal, rose-breasted and evening grosbeaks, purple finch, common redpoll, pine siskin, American goldfinch, yellow-bellied sapsucker

Cover and/or Nesting: red-bellied, hairy, and downy woodpeckers; common flicker, white-breasted nuthatch, red-eyed vireo, yellow warbler, American robin, American redstart

Food (seeds), Cover, and Nesting: black-capped and Carolina chickadees, northern oriole

Food (browse): white-tailed deer, fox squirrel, beaver, white-footed mouse

Hydrology

Indicator status: Facultative wetland –

Salinity: fresh water; less than 0.5 ppt

Tidal zone:

Nontidal regime: irregularly to seasonally saturated (up to approximately 25% of the growing season)

Environmental Concern Inc.

Viburnum lentago
Nannyberry, Sweet viburnum, Sheepberry

Characteristics
Broad-leaved, deciduous tree

GROWTH
Rate: fast; 2 to 2.5 ft. per yr.
Spreads by suckers

PLANTING
Forms available: bare root, container, balled and
burlapped

HABITAT
Community: forested seasonal wetlands
stream and swamp edges

Distribution: western Quebec to Manitoba, south to
Georgia and Mississippi

Shade: tolerates full shade

NOTES
Fairly insensitive to wind or ice damage
pH preference = 6.0 - 7.5
Forms dense thickets through sucker production

Appearance
Height: 20 to 35 ft.
Aerial spread: 10 to 35 ft.
Flower color: white, in flat-topped clusters
Flowering period: mid- through late May
Fruit description: yellow or red, ripening to black
Fruiting period: early September through
early December

Wildlife Benefits
Potential Benefits and Species Served

Food (fruit): common flicker, American robin, eastern
bluebird, cedar waxwing, rose-breasted grosbeak,
purple finch, pileated woodpecker, grouse, wild
turkey, rabbit, chipmunk, squirrel

Food (fruit) and Cover: ruffed grouse, bobwhite, ring-
necked pheasant, hermit thrush

Food (fruit, twigs, foliage, bark): deer, beaver

Food, Cover, and Nesting: gray catbird

Berries last through fall, into winter

Hydrology

Indicator status: Facultative

Salinity: fresh water; less than 0.5 ppt

Tidal zone:

Nontidal regime: seasonally inundated or saturated
(approximately 13 to 25% of the growing
season)

WETLAND PLANT SUPPLIERS

The following is a list of nurseries which are known to carry wetland plant materials. Most are nurseries from the northeastern United States but some from outside the region have been included. This list is not necessarily complete and other nurseries decide to include wetland plants in their stock on an on-going basis. If species cannot be found at these nurseries, others should be contacted.

Bigelow Nurseries
P.O. Box 718
Northborough, MA 01532
Phone: (508) 845-2143

Blackledge River Nursery
Rt. 354
Salem, CT 06415
Phone: (203) 859-2428

Buddies Nursery
P.O. Box 14
Birdsboro, PA 19508
Phone: (215) 582-2410
FAX: (215) 779-8090

Carolina Seacoast Beach Plants
Professional Park Suite 8
P.O. Box 1194
Morehead City, NC 28557-1194
Phone: (919) 240-2415

Country Wetlands Nursery, Ltd.
Box 126
Muskego, WI 53150
Phone: (414) 679-1268

Ecoscience
RD 4 Box 4294
Moscow, PA 18444
(717) 842-7631

Environmental Concern Inc.
P.O. Box P, 210 West Chew Ave.
St. Michaels, MD 21663
Phone: (410) 745-9620
FAX: (410) 745-3517

Environmental Consultants, Inc.
P.O. Box 3198
Suffolk, VA 23434
Phone: (804) 539-4833

Ernst Crownvetch Farms
R.D. 5, Box 806
Meadville, PA 16335
Phone: (814) 425-7276
FAX: (814) 425-2228

Gardens of the Blue Ridge
P.O. Box 10
Pineola, NC 28662
Phone: (704) 733-2417

Green Biz Nursery & Landscaping, Inc.
P.O. Box 64995
Fayetteville, NC 28306
Phone: 1-800-848-6634

Kester's Wild Game Food Nurseries, Inc.
P.O. Box 516
Omro, WI 54963
Phone: (414) 685-2929

L.A. Brochu & Son Nurseries, Inc.
121 Commercial Street
Concord, NH 03301
Phone: (603) 224-4350
FAX: (603) 226-0869

LaFayette Home Nursery, Inc.
R.R. 1, Box 1A
LaFayette, IL 61449
Phone: (309) 995-3311
FAX: (309) 995-3909

Lilypons Water Gardens
6800 Lilypons Road
P.O. Box 10
Buckeystown, MD 21717-0010
Phone: (301) 874-5133
FAX: (301) 874-2959

Millican Nurseries, Inc.
R.R. 3, Box 3756
Chichester, NH 03263
(603) 435-6660

North Creek Nurseries
R.R. #2, Box 33
Landenberg, PA 19350
Phone: (215) 255-0100

Pinelands Nursery
R.R. 1, Box 12
Island Road
Columbus, NJ 08022
Phone: (609) 291-9486
FAX: (609) 298-6846

Prairie Ridge Nursery
R.R. 2
9738 Overland Road
Mt. Horeb, WI 53572
Phone: (608) 437-5245

Princeton Nurseries
P.O. Box 191
Princeton, NJ 08542
Phone: (609) 924-1776

The Salt and the Earth
P.O. Box 51
Deltaville, VA 23043
Phone: (804) 776-6324

Southern Tier Consulting, Inc.
P.O. Box 550
Portville, NY 14770
Phone: (716) 933-6169

Squirrel Creek Nursery
R.R. #2, Box 273-C
Ulster, PA 18850
Phone: (717) 596-4514

Sylva Native Nursery and Seed Co., Inc.
RD 2, Box 1033
New Freedom, PA 17349
Phone: (410) 560-2288
FAX: (410) 560-2285

Sylvan Nursery Inc.
1028 Horseneck Road
South Westport, MA 02790
Phone: (508) 636-4573
FAX: (508) 636-3397

Van Hoose's Nursery
Rt. 1, Box 1760
West Point, VA 23181
(804) 539-4833

Waterford Gardens
74 East Allendale Road
Saddle River, NJ 07458
Phone: (201) 327-0721
FAX: (201) 327-0684

Weston Nurseries, Inc.
E. Main St. (Rt. 135)
P.O. Box 186
Hopkinton, MA 01748-0186
Phone: (508) 435-3414
FAX: (508) 435-3274

Wicklein's Water Gardens
1820 Cromwell Bridge Road
Baltimore, MD 21234
Phone: (410) 823-1335

Wild Earth Native Plant Nursery
49 Mead Avenue
Freehold, NJ 07728
Phone: (908) 780-5661

Wildlife Nurseries
P.O. Box 2724
Oshkosh, WI 54903
Phone: (414) 231-3780

William Tricker, Inc.
7125 Tanglewood Drive
Independence, OH 44131
Phone: (216) 524-3491
FAX: (216) 524-6688

REFERENCES

Allen, H.H. and C.V. Klimas. 1986. Reservoir Shoreline Revegetation Guidelines. Technical Report E-86-13. U.S. Army Engineer Waterways Experiment Station, Vicksburg, Mississippi. 87 pp.

Armitage, A.M. 1989. Herbaceous Perennial Plants: A Treatise on their Identification, Culture, and Garden Attributes. Varsity Press, Inc., Athens, Georgia. 646 pp.

Barnhart, R.K. 1986. The American Heritage Dictionary of Science. Houghton Mifflin Company, Boston. 740 pp.

Bartoldus, C.C. 1990. Revegetation and Production in a Constructed Freshwater Tidal Marsh. Ph.D. Thesis. George Mason University, Fairfax, Virginia. 225 pp.

Bartoldus, C.C. and F.D. Heliotis. 1989. Factors affecting the survival of planted material in the Marley Creek constructed freshwater tidal marsh, Maryland, pp. 1-5. In Transportation Research Record 1224. Transportation Research Board, National Research Council, Washington, D.C.

Beal, E.O. 1977. A Manual of Marsh and Aquatic Vascular Plants of North Carolina with Habitat Data. The North Carolina Agricultural Research Service. Raleigh, North Carolina.

Best, R.G. and K.L. Erwin. 1984. Effects of hydroperiod on survival and growth of tree seedlings in a phosphate surface-mined reclaimed wetland, pp. 221-225. In D. Graves (Ed.), Symposium on Surface Mining, Hydrology, Sedimentology, and Reclamation. University of Kentucky, Lexington, Kentucky.

Bir, R.E. 1992. Native Azaleas. Horticulture LXX:5:52-55.

Brandt, K. and K.C. Ewel. 1989. Ecology and Management of Cypress Swamps: A Review. Bulletin 252. Florida Cooperative Extension Service, University of Florida. 19 pp.

Brinson, M.M., B.L. Swift, R.C. Plantico, and J.S. Barclay. 1981. Riparian Ecosystems: Their Ecology and Status. FWS/OBS-81/17. U.S. Fish and Wildlife Service, Kearneysville, West Virginia. 155 pp.

Broadfoot, W.M. and H.L. Williston. 1973. Flooding effects on southern forests. Journal of Forestry 71:584-587

Broome, S.W., E.D. Seneca, and W.W. Woodhouse, Jr. 1982. Establishing brackish marshes on graded upland sites in North Carolina. Wetlands 2:152-178.

Brown, M.L. and R.G. Brown. 1984. Herbaceous Plants of Maryland. Port City Press, Baltimore, Maryland. 1127 pp.

Brown, R.G. and M.L. Brown. 1972. Woody Plants of Maryland. Port City Press, Baltimore, Maryland. 347 pp.

Cowardin, L.M., V. Carter, F.C. Golet, and E.T. LaRoe. 1979. Classification of Wetlands and Deepwater Habitats of the United States. FWS/OBS-79/31. U.S. Fish and Wildlife Service. Washington, D.C. 131 pp.

Cox, D.D. 1985. Common Flowering Plants of the Northeast. State University of New York Press, Albany, New York. 418 pp.

Degraaf, R.M. and G.M. Witman. 1979. Trees, Shrubs, and Vines for Attracting Birds: A Manual for the Northeast. University of Massachusetts Press, Amherst, Massachusetts. 194 pp.

Duncan, W.H. and M.B. Duncan. 1987. The Smithsonian Guide to Seaside Plants of the Gulf and Atlantic Coasts from Louisiana to Massachusetts, exclusive of Lower Peninsular Florida. Smithsonian Institution Press. 409 pp.

Elakovich, S.D. and J.W. Wooten. 1989. Allelopathic Aquatic Plants for Aquatic Plant Management: A Feasibility Study. Technical Report A-89-2. U.S. Army Corp of Engineers, Environmental Laboratory, Vicksburg, Mississippi. 27 pp. + Appendix.

Eleuterius, L.N. 1990. Tidal Marsh Plants. Pelican Publishing Company, Gretna, Louisiana. 168 pp.

Elias, T.S. 1987. The Complete Trees of North America: A Field Guide and Natural History. Gramercy Publishing Company, New York, New York. 948 pp.

Environmental Concern Inc. Plants for Landscaping Shores, Ponds and Other Wet Areas. St. Michaels, Maryland. 5 pp.

Environmental Concern Inc. Shrubs and Trees for Wildlife Habitat Development. St. Michaels, Maryland. 7 pp.

Environmental Laboratory. 1978. Wetland Habitat Development with Dredged Material: Engineering and Plant Propagation. Technical Report DS-78-16. U.S. Army Engineer Waterways Experiment Station, Vicksburg, Mississippi. 107 pp. + Appendices.

Environmental Laboratory. 1987. Corps of Engineers Wetlands Delineation Manual. Technical Report Y-87-1. U.S. Army Waterways Experiment Station. Vicksburg, Mississippi.

Faber, P.M., E. Keller, A. Sands, and B.M. Massey. 1989. The Ecology of Riparian Habitats of the Southern California Coastal Region: A Community Profile. Biological Report 85(7.27). U.S. Fish and Wildlife Service, Washington, D.C. 152 pp.

Fernald, M.L. 1987. Grays Manual of Botany: Eighth Edition. Dioscorides Press, Portland, Oregon. 1632 pp.

Foote, L.E. and S.B. Jones, Jr. 1989. Native Shrubs and Woody Vines of the Southeast. Timber Press, Portland, Oregon. 199 pp.

Frost, I.G., P.E. Johnson, J.R. McClain, S.C. Russell, E.D. Whedbee. 1989. Draft Wetland Compensation Report. Commonwealth of Virginia, Virginia Department of Transportation. 84 pp. + Appendix.

Garbisch, E.W. 1986. Highways & Wetlands: Compensating Wetland Losses. Contract Report DOT-FH-11-9442. Federal Highway Administration, Office of Implementation, McLean, Virginia.

Garbisch, E.W. and L.B. Coleman. 1978. Tidal freshwater marsh establishment in upper Chesapeake Bay; *Pontederia cordata* and *Peltandra virginica*, pp. 285-298. In R.E. Good, D.F. Whigham, and R.L. Simpson (Eds.), Freshwater Wetlands: Ecological Processes & Management Potential. Academic Press, New York, New York.

Gilbert, T., T. King, B. Barnett. 1981. An Assessment of Wetland Habitat Establishment at a Central Florida Phosphate Mine Site. FWS/OBS-81/38. U.S. Fish and Wildlife Service, Atlanta, Georgia. 95 pp.

Gleason, H.A. 1952. The New Britton and Brown Illustrated Flora of the Northeastern United States and Adjacent Canada. Hafner Press for the New York Botanical Garden, New York, New York.

Godfrey, R.K. and J.W. Wooten. 1979. Aquatic and Wetland Plants of Southeastern United States: Monocotyledons. The University of Georgia Press, Athens, Georgia. 712 pp.

Godfrey, R.K. and J.W. Wooten. 1981. Aquatic and Wetland Plants of Southeastern United States: Dicotyledons. The University of Georgia Press, Athens, Georgia. 933 pp.

Gouin, F.R. Desirable Soil pH and Salt Tolerance of Ornamental Plants. Cooperative Extension Service: Horticulture Production. University of Maryland, College Park, Maryland.

Gunderson, L.H., J.R. Stenberg, and A.K. Herndon. 1988. Tolerance of five hardwood species to flooding regimes, pp. 119-132. In D.A. Wilcox (Ed.), Interdisciplinary Approaches to Freshwater Wetlands Research. Michigan State University Press, East Lansing, Michigan.

Guntenspergen, G.R., F. Stearns, and J.A. Kadlec. 1989. Wetland vegetation, pp. 73-88. In D.A. Hammer (Ed.), Constructed Wetlands for Wastewater Treatment. Lewis Publishers, Chelsea, Michigan.

Haynes, R.J., J.A. Allen, and E.C. Pendleton. 1988. Reestablishment of Bottomland Hardwood Forests on Disturbed Sites: An Annotated Bibliography. Biological Report 88(42). U.S. Fish and Wildlife Service, Washington, D.C.

Hightshoe, G.L. 1988. Native Trees, Shrubs, and Vines for Urban and Rural America: A Planting Design Manual for Environmental Designers. Van Nostrand Reinhold, New York, New York. 819 pp.

Hitchcock, A.S. 1971. Manual of the Grasses of the United States (Volumes I and II): Second Edition. Agnes Chase (Ed.). Dover Publications, New York, New York. 1051 pp.

Hotchkiss, N. 1972. Common Marsh, Underwater & Floating-leaved Plants of the United States and Canada. Dover Publications, New York, New York. 223 pp.

Hurley, L.M. 1990. Field Guide to the Submerged Aquatic Vegetation of Chesapeake Bay. U.S. Fish and Wildlife Service, Annapolis, Maryland. 51 pp.

Illinois Department of Conservation. 1981. Illinois Plants for Habitat Restoration: Commercial Availability, Characteristics and Fish and Wildlife Utilization. Illinois Department of Conservation Mining Program, Springfield, Illinois. 61 pp.

Jones, S.B., Jr. and L.E. Foote. 1990. Gardening with Native Wild Flowers. Timber Press, Portland, Oregon. 195 pp.

Josselyn, M.N. 1983. The Ecology of San Francisco Bay Tidal Marshes: A Community Profile. FWS/OBS-83/23. U.S. Fish and Wildlife Service, Washington, D.C. 102 pp.

Josselyn, M.N. and J.W. Buchholz. 1984. Marsh Restoration in San Francisco Bay: A Guide to Design & Planning. Technical Report #3. Tiburon Center for Environmental Studies. San Francisco State University. 104 pp.

Kadlec, J.A. and W.A. Wentz. 1974. State-of-the-Art Survey and Evaluation of Marsh Plant Establishment Techniques: Induced and Natural, Volume I: Report of Research. Contract Report D-74-9. U.S. Army Engineer Waterways Experiment Station, Vicksburg, Mississippi.

Kantrud, H.A. 1990. Sago Pondweed *(Potamogeton pectinatus* L.): A Literature Review. Resource Publication 176. U.S. Fish and Wildlife Service, Washington, D.C. 89 pp.

Kartesz, J.T. and R. Kartesz. 1980. A Synonymized Checklist of the Vascular Flora of the United States, Canada, and Greenland. The University of North Carolina Press, Chapel Hill, North Carolina. 498 pp.

Kelley, J.R., Jr. 1991. Chufa Biology and Management, Section 13.4.18. In D.H. Cross (compiler), Waterfowl Management Handbook. U.S. Fish and Wildlife Service. Leaflet 13. Washington, D.C.

Knutson, P.L. and W.W. Woodhouse, Jr. 1983. Shore Stabilization with Salt Marsh Vegetation. Special Report No. 9. U.S. Army Corps of Engineers, Coastal Engineering Research Center, Fort Belvoir, VA 96 pp.

Korschgen, C.E. and W.L. Green. 1988. American Wildcelery *(Vallisneria americana)*: Ecological Considerations for Restoration. Fish and Wildlife Technical Report 19. U.S. Department of the Interior, Fish and Wildlife Service, Washington, D.C. 24 pp.

Kroeger, S.R. 1990. Wetland Vegetation Establishment in L-Lake. Savannah River Ecology Laboratory, Aiken, South Carolina. 33 pp. + Appendices.

Laderman, A.D. 1989. The Ecology of Atlantic White Cedar Wetlands: A Community Profile. Biological Report 85(7.21). U.S. Fish and Wildlife Service, Washington, D.C. 114 pp.

Landin, M.C., J.W. Webb, and P.L. Knutson. 1989. Long-Term Monitoring of Eleven Corps of Engineers Habitat Development Field Sites Built of Dredged Material, 1974-1987. Technical Report D-89-1. U.S. Army Engineer Waterways Experiment Station, Vicksburg, Mississippi. 192 pp. + Appendix.

Lawton, B.P. 1990. Plant health: a vital link. American Nurseryman August 15:76-84.

Lefor, M.W. 1987. *Phalaris arundinacea* (reed canary grass - Gramineae) as a hydrophyte in Essex, Connecticut, USA. Environmental Management 11:6:771-773.

Lemberger, J. 1981. Wildlife Nurseries Plant Catalog (What Brings Them In). Wildlife Nurseries, Oshkosh, Wisconsin. 32 pp.

Levine, D.A. and D.E. Willard. 1989. Regional analysis of fringe wetlands in the midwest: creation and restoration, pp. 305-332. In J.A. Kusler and M.E. Kentula (Eds.), Wetland Creation and Restoration: The Status of the Science, Vol. I. U.S. Environmental Protection Agency, Corvallis, Oregon.

Lewis, R.R., III. 1989. Creation and restoration of coastal plain wetlands in Florida, pp. 73-101. In J.A. Kusler and M.E. Kentula (Eds.), Wetland Creation and Restoration: The Status of the Science Vol. I. U.S. Environmental Protection Agency, Corvallis, Oregon.

Lindeman, W. and J.R. Wilt, Jr. 1988. Effectiveness of Mitigation Techniques at the Alafia River Crossing. Florida Department of Transportation, Environmental Research. 21 pp.

Martin, A.C., H.S. Zim, and A.L. Nelson. 1951. American Wildlife & Plants: A Guide to Wildlife Food Habits. Dover Publications, New York, New York. 500 pp.

McKnight, S.J., D. Hook, G.O. Langdon, and R.L. Johnson. 1981. Flood tolerance and related characteristics of trees of the bottomland forests of the southern United States, pp. 29-69. In J.R. Clark and J. Benforado (Eds.), Wetlands of Bottomland Hardwood Forests: Proceedings of a Workshop on Bottomland Hardwood Forest Wetlands of the Southeastern United States. Elsevier Scientific Publishing Company, Amsterdam, The Netherlands.

Miller, H. and S. Lamb. 1985. Oaks of North America. Naturegraph Publishers, Happy Camp, California.

Mitsch, W.J. and J.G. Gosselink. 1986. Wetlands. Van Nostrand Reinhold Company, New York. 539 pp.

Newling, C.J. 1990. Restoration of bottomland hardwood forests in the Lower Mississippi Valley. Restoration & Management Notes 8(1):23-28.

Odum, W.E., T.J. Smith, J.K. Hoover, and C.C. McIvor. 1984. The Ecology of Tidal Freshwater Marshes of the United States East Coast: A Community Profile. FWS/OBS-83-17. U.S. Fish and Wildlife Service, Washington, D.C. 177 pp.

Owen, C.R., Q.J. Carpenter, and C.B. DeWitt. 1989. Evaluation of Three Wetland Restorations Associated With Highway Projects. Transportation Policy Studies Institute, Wisconsin Department of Transportation. Madison, Wisconsin. 89 pp.

Palmer, E.L. and H.S. Fowler. 1975. Fieldbook of Natural History: Second Edition. McGraw-Hill Book Company, New York. 779 pp.

Peterson, L.N. 1987. Wild celery transplanted (Wisconsin). Restoration & Management Notes 5(1):35-36.

Phillips, R.C. 1982. Seagrass meadows, pp. 173-210. In R.R. Lewis, III (Ed.), Creation and Restoration of Coastal Plant Communities. CRC Press, Boca Raton, Florida.

Pierce, G.J. 1990. Freshwater Emergent Marsh Restoration. Wetlands Development and Restoration. Corps of Engineers Training Management Division, Huntsville, Alabama.

Platts, W.S., C. Armour, G.D. Booth, M. Bryant, J.L. Bufford, P. Cuplin, S. Jensen, G.W. Lienkaemper, G.W. Minshall, S.B. Monsen, R.L. Nelson, J.R. Sedell, and J.S. Tuhy. 1987. Methods for Evaluating Riparian Habitats with Applications to Management. General Technical Report INT-221. U.S. Department of Agriculture Forest Service, Ogden, Utah. 177 pp.

Plewa, F.R. 1987. A Guide to Wetland Plantings in Pennsylvania and Recommended Approaches to Establishing Vegetative Cover. Special Project Report No. 87-1. U.S. Fish and Wildlife Service, State College, Pennsylvania.

Reed, P.B. Jr. 1988. National List of Plant Species That Occur in Wetlands: Northeast (Region 1). Biological Report 88(26.1). U.S. Fish and Wildlife Service. Washington, D.C. 111 pp.

Ross, W.M. and R.H. Chabreck. 1972. Factors affecting the growth and survival of natural and planted stands of *Scirpus olneyi*, pp. 178-188. In A.L. Mitchell (Ed.), Proceedings of the Twenty-sixth Annual Conference. Southeastern Association of Game and Fish Commissioners, Knoxville, Tennessee.

Schopmeyer, C.S. 1974. Seeds of Woody Plants in the United States. Agriculture Handbook No. 450. Forest Service, U.S. Department of Agriculture, Washington, D.C. 883 pp.

Shisler, J.K. 1989. Creation and restoration of coastal wetlands of the northeastern United States, pp. 145-174. In J.A. Kusler and M.E. Kentula (Eds.), Wetland Creation and Restoration: The Status of the Science, Vol. I. U.S. Environmental Protection Agency, Corvallis, Oregon.

Silberhorn, G.M. 1982. Common Plants of the Mid-Atlantic Coast, A Field Guide. The Johns Hopkins University Press, Baltimore, Maryland. 256 pp.

Southern Tier Consulting and Ecology & Environment. 1987. Wetland Demonstration Project. Allegheny River Floodplain. New York Department of Transportation.

Steenis, J.H. 1950. Waterfowl habitat improvement on Reelfoot Lake. Journal of the Tennessee Academy of Science 25:56-75.

Stephenson, M., G. Turner, P. Pope, J. Colt, A. Knight, and G. Tchobanaglous. 1980. The Use and Potential of Aquatic Species for Wastewater Treatment. Publication No. 65 - Appendix A: The Environmental Requirements of Aquatic Plants. California State Water Resources Control Board. Sacramento, California. 655 pp.

Stout, J.P. 1984. The Ecology of Irregularly Flooded Salt Marshes of the Northeastern Gulf of Mexico: A Community Profile. Biological Report 85(7.1). U.S. Fish and Wildlife Service, Washington, D.C. 98 pp.

Strausbaugh, P.D. and E.L. Core. Flora of West Virginia, Second Edition. Seneca Books, Grantsville, West Virginia. 1079 pp.

Teal, J.M. 1986. The Ecology of Regularly Flooded Salt Marshes of New England: A Community Profile. Biological Report 85(7.4). U.S. Fish and Wildlife Service, Washington, D.C. 61 pp.

Thayer, G.W., W.J. Kenworthy, and M.S. Fonseca. 1984. The Ecology of Eelgrass Meadows of the Atlantic Coast: A Community Profile. FWS/OBS-84/02. U.S. Fish and Wildlife Service, Washington, D.C. 147 pp.

Thompson, D.Q. 1989. Control of Purple Loosestrife, Section 13.4.11. In D.H. Cross (compiler), Waterfowl Management Handbook. Leaflet 13. U.S. Fish and Wildlife Service, Washington, D.C.

Thorhaug, A. 1990. Restoration of mangroves and sea grasses - economic benefits for fisheries and mariculture, pp. 265-281. In J.J. Berger (Eds.), Environmental Restoration: Science and Strategies for Restoring the Earth. Island Press, Washington, D.C.

Tiner, R.W., Jr. 1987. A Field Guide to Coastal Wetland Plants of the Northeastern United States. The University of Massachusetts Press, Amherst, Massachusetts. 285 pp.

Tiner, R.W., Jr. 1988. Field Guide to Nontidal Wetland Identification. Maryland Department of Natural Resources and U.S. Fish and Wildlife Service, Annapolis, Maryland and Newton Corner, Massachusetts. 283 pp.

Vogl, R.J. 1966. Salt-marsh vegetation of upper Newport Bay, California. Ecology 47(1):80-87.

Whitlow, T.H. and R.W. Harris. 1979. Flood Tolerance in Plants: A State-of-the-Art Review. Technical Report E-79-2. U.S. Army Engineer Waterways Experiment Station, Vicksburg, Mississippi. 257 pp.

Wilcox, D.A., N.B. Pavlovic, and M.L. Mueggler. 1985. Selected ecological characteristics of *Scirpus cyperinus* and its role as an invader of disturbed wetlands. Wetlands 5:87-97.

Woodhouse, W.W., Jr. and P.L. Knutson. 1982. Atlantic coastal marshes, pp. 45-70. In R.R. Lewis, III (Ed.), Creation and Restoration of Coastal Plant Communities. CRC Press, Boca Raton, Florida.

Zedler, J.B. 1984. Salt Marsh Restoration: A Guidebook for Southern California. California Sea Grant College Program, La Jolla, California. 46 pp.

Zieman, J.C. and R.T. Zieman. 1989. The Ecology of the Seagrass Meadows of the West Coast of Florida: A Community Profile. Biological Report 85(7.25). U.S. Fish and Wildlife Service, Washington, D.C. 155 pp.

INDEX

Gum
    Black   152
    Sour   152
Hackberry   147
Hardstem bulrush   88
Hay, Salt marsh   100
Hazel alder   111
Heart's ease   79
Hibiscus, Marsh   56
Hibiscus moscheutos   *2, 56*
High tide bush   125
Highbush blueberry   136
Highbush cranberry   138
Highwater grass   100
Holly
    Deciduous   121
    Inkberry   122
    Swamp   123
    Winterberry   123
Honeysuckle, Purple   131
Hornwort   9
Hydrocotyle umbellata   *57*
Ilex
    decidua   *121*
    glabra   *122*
    verticillata   *123*
indicator status   4
Indigo bush   112
    False   112
Inkberry   122
intertidal zone   5
inundation   6
Iris
    pseudacorus   *58*
    versicolor   *59*
Iris
    Blue water   59
    Yellow water   58
Itea virginica   *124*
Iva frutescens   *125*
Jack in the pulpit, Small   30
Juncus
    balticus   *60*
    effusus   *61*
    roemerianus   *62*
    tenuis   *63*
    torreyi   *64*
Juneberry, Oblong-leaf   144
King-cup   35
Knotted spike rush   47
Kosteletzkya virginica   *65*
Lady's thumb   79
Lake sedge   38
Leersia oryzoides   *66*

Lemna minor   *11*
Lesser bur-reed   96
Leucothoe racemosa   *126*
Lily
    Fragrant water   14
    Pond   14
    White water   14
    Yellow water   69
Lindera benzoin   *127*
Liquidambar styraciflua   *151*
Lizard tail   87
Lobelia cardinalis   *5, 67*
Loblolly pine   154
Long-leaved pond plant   16
Loosestrife, Purple   68
Lotus   13
Lowland broom sedge   28
Lythrum salicaria   *68*
Lythrum, Spike   68
Magnolia, Sweetbay   128
Magnolia virginiana   *128*
Mallow, Seashore   65
Manna, Floating   54
Mannagrass   54
    American   52
    Eastern   54
    Floating   53
    Fowl   55
    Nerved   55
    Rattlesnake   51
Maple
    Ash-leaved   141
    Red   142
    River   143
    Silver   143
    Soft   143
    White   143
Marigold, Marsh   35
Marsh elder   125
Marsh fern   104
Marsh hibiscus   56
Marsh marigold   35
Marsh smartweed   77, 80
Marsh spike rush   49
Meadow fern   104
Mild water pepper   77
Milkweed, Swamp   31
Mud plantain   27
Myrica
    cerifera   *129*
    pensylvanica   *130*
Myrtle
    Sea   115
    Sweet   25
    Wax   129

Nannyberry   165
Narrow-leaved cattail   105
Nasturtium officinale   *12*
Needlerush, Black   62
Nelumbo lutea   *13*
Nerved mannagrass   55
Netted chain fern   107
New England aster   32
New York fern   103
Northern white cedar   163
Nuphar
    advena   *69*
    luteum   *69*
Nutgrass, Yellow   44
Nutsedge, Yellow   44
Nymphea odorata   *14*
Nyssa sylvatica   *152*
Oak
    Pin   159
    Possum   158
    Spanish   159
    Swamp white   157
    Water   158
    Willow   160
Oblong-leaf Juneberry   144
Oldfield birch   146
Olney threesquare   89
Olney's bulrush   89
Onoclea sensibilis   *70*
Orache   33
    Marsh   33
Osmunda
    cinnamomea   *71*
    regalis   *72*
Pacific glasswort   86
Panicum virgatum   *73*
Parsnip, Water   95
Peltandra virginica   *4, 74*
Pennsylvania smartweed   78
Pennywort, Water   57
Pepper, Mild water   77
Pepperbush, Sweet   117
perennial   2
Perennial glasswort   86
Perennial pickleweed   86
persistent   2
Phalaris arundinacea   *75*
Phragmites australis   *76*
Pickerelweed   81
Pickleweed   86
    Perennial   86
Pin oak   159
Pine
    Loblolly   154
    Pitch   153

NOTES

NOTES

NOTES